# CHINA
## ILLUSTRATED

# CHINA ILLUSTRATED

## Western Views of the Middle Kingdom

Arthur Hacker

Published by Tuttle Publishing,
an imprint of Periplus Editions (HK) Ltd

Text and illustrations © 2004 Arthur Hacker

Library of Congress Control Number: 2004101805
ISBN 0-8048-3519-5

All rights reserved.

Book design: mind, London and Arthur Hacker
Printed in Singapore

Distributed by:
*North America, Latin America and Europe*
Tuttle Publishing, 364 Innovation Drive,
North Clarendon, VT 05759-9436, USA
Tel: (802) 773 8930; Fax: (802) 526 2778
E-mail: info@tuttlepublishing.com
http://www.tuttlepublishing.com

*Japan*
Tuttle Publishing, Yaekari Building, 3F,
5-4-12 Osaki, Shinagawa-ku, Tokyo, 141-0032
Tel: (03) 5437 0171; Fax: (03) 5437 0755
E-mail: tuttle-sales@gol.com

*Asia Pacific*
Berkeley Books Pte Ltd, 130 Joo Seng Road
#06-01/03, Singapore 368357
Tel: (65) 6280 1330; Fax: (65) 6280 6290
E-mail: inquiries@periplus.com.sg
http://www.periplus.com

*Author's Note*
This book is designed to be easily read by those not familiar with the intricacies of *pinyin* spelling and pronunciation, which was adopted after the events in the book took place. A modified Wade-Giles system has been used to romanize Chinese personal and place names in order to be consistent with the terminology in the primary sources. For the convenience of the Chinese reader, the *pinyin* word appears in brackets after the traditional English spelling of the name, e.g. Peking (Beijing), Canton (Guangzhou) and Chou En-lai (Zhou En-lai), on its first occurrence in each chapter.

*Acknowledgments*
I would like to thank everybody who helped with this book for their support, enthusiasm and encouragement, especially Jonathan Sharp, the former Bureau Chief of Reuters, Peking, who kindly looked over and corrected my manuscript; China and computer experts Tim McGuire and Jessie Chong for their technical help and useful advice; Jonathan and Vicky Wattis of Wattis Fine Art whose knowledge of old China maps, prints and photographs was invaluable; enthusiastic fellow historians like Phillip Bruce who loaned me books; and old China hands like David Roads who had fascinating tales to tell.

*Page 1*: Chinese opera mask on a cigarette card, 1920s; *Page 2*: The Hadamen Gate in the Tartar Wall in 1934. The gate connected the Chinese and Tartar Cities. During the Ching (Qing) dynasty, the ruling Manchus and most Westerners lived in the Tartar City. The foreign legations were close to this gate. *Page 3*: A popular Victorian wood engraving of a Chinese girl dancing. *Pages 4–5*: Construction work on the Great Wall of China began during the seventh century BC. It is over 3,000 miles long. Romantics claim that it can be seen from the moon in spite of the wall being, on average, only 12 feet wide. *Page 6*: A Chinese actor playing the part of an enraged military officer during a theatrical performance put on for Lord Macartney during his mission to China. This engraving is from a sketch by William Alexander which he drew on 19 December 1793 during the performance.

London Published Aug.t 13th 1801, by G. and W. Nicol Pallmall.

# Contents

| | |
|---|---|
| **Foreword** | **8** |
| **Introduction** | **10** |

**Chapter 1**
**East is East and West is West (1557–1860)**     **16**

Foreign Devils from the West 22
Matteo Ricci and the First Jesuits in China 28
The John Company and Others 32
The Swedish East India Company 38
The Embassies That Failed 42
An Artist on the Grand Canal 44
The Interlopers and Taipans 48
Laboriously Vile 54
An American at Canton 58
Commissioner Lin and Captain Elliot 62
Two Irishmen 64
The Pirates of the South China Sea 68
Harry Parkes and the Arrow War 74
Old Maps of China 78
Eighteenth and Nineteenth Century Prints of China 84

**Chapter 2**
**The Empire of Opportunity and the Treaty Ports (1860–1894)**     **92**

The Beginning of the Missionary Invasion 100
The Taiping Rebellion (1851–1864) 104
The Ever-Victorious Army 108
Sir Robert Hart of the Chinese Imperial Maritime Customs 110
Ching Peking 112
The First Treaty Ports 118
The Great China Tea Race 128
Transport in the Middle Kingdom 132
Footbinding: Ching Dynasty Fashion Victims 138
Through China with a Camera (1868–1872) 142
A Country of Clubs 150

**Chapter 3**
**The End of Empire and the New Republic (1894–1918)**     **152**

Weihaiwei: The Scramble for Concessions 158
Mortimer Menpes: Whistler's Disciple 162

Tzu Hsi: The Dragon Empress 166
The Boxer Rebellion: The Siege of the Legations 170
The Odd Couple: Sir Edmund Backhouse and Dr G. E. Morrison 174
Port Arthur: The Russian Concession in Manchuria 176
Life before Television in Expatriate China 178
A Touch of Satire in Ching China 182
The Double Tenth 1911 and the Fall of the House of Ching 184
A Camel in the Chinese Customs Service 188
The Maker of Heavenly Trousers 192

**Chapter 4**
**Turbulence and Decadence (1919–1927)**     **196**

The Grandeur of the Three Gorges 202
Sir Reginald Johnston: Tutor to the Last Emperor 206
The Man Who Captured the Great Wall of China 208
Shanghai: The Days of No Tomorrow 212
Cigarette Advertising in the Great Tobacco War 214
Picture Postcards of China 218
Sun Yat-sen's Bodyguard: General Two-Gun Cohen 222
The Shanghai Volunteers 226
The Incident on the Blue Express and Other Kidnappings 230
The White Russians 232
The Northern Expedition and Chiang Kai-shek's Coup 234

**Chapter 5**
**Nationalistic China at Peace and War (1928–1941)**     **238**

The Pursuit of Wealth 244
Carl Crow and His 400 Million Customers 248
The Westernized Chinese 252
The Gentle Art of Making Fun 256
The Great Espionage Epidemic 258
Photographers of the 1920s and 1930s 260
The Japanese Attack on Shanghai (1932) 270
The Lull and the Storm 274
The Media Circus 276
The Rape of Nanking (December 1937) 280
Epilogue 282

| | |
|---|---|
| **Bibliography** | **284** |
| **Index** | **285** |

# FOREWORD

In most illustrated histories the written text precedes the visual depiction. Arthur Hacker's representation of late imperial and modern Chinese history is unique because it proceeds from images to narrative. Some of the maps, engravings, drawings, paintings, photographs and posters are familiar to us. But the majority of pictures in this lavishly designed volume are fresh and new, providing us with a colorful appreciation of the social landscape of China and with a striking sense of the dramatic changes that took place between the Opium Wars of the nineteenth century and the revolutionary movements of the twentieth.

This is not a straightforward textbook of modern Chinese history. The author gives a remarkably succinct introduction to each stage of his narrative, and then proceeds to group illustrations around a singular topic or theme: tribute missions, foreign traders at Canton, South China pirates, the Taiping Rebellion, life in the treaty ports, popular customs, the scramble for concessions, the Boxers, the late Ching court, Sun Yat-sen's Canadian bodyguard, White Russians in Shanghai, revolutionary movements, bandits, espionage, the Japanese attack on Nanking, and so on, all the way down to the rise of the People's Republic. Much of this is, quite literally, picturesque. All of it is strongly interactive, so that the reader moves readily from text to image and back again to text.

The author's vantage point is a Western perspective, which is only natural given the pictorial materials available to him: whether early Dutch engravings of Jesuits, William Alexander's sketches of life along the Grand Canal at the time of Lord Macartney's embassy to the Chien Lung court in 1793, Auguste Borget's lithographs of Canton during the heyday of the East India Company, or John Thomson's photographic portraits of the imperial viceroys of the 1870s who sought to strengthen China by building modern arsenals and shipyards. There are also the familiar grotesqueries: women with bound feet, the eccentric caricatures of Daniele Varè's *Maker of Heavenly Trousers*, dog-eating warlords and sword-wielding executioners.

As the historian James Hevia has recently pointed out, these depictions amounted to a kind of discursive colonization of the Chinese, a racist process rendered all the more insidious because it subversively made the Chinese deprecate themselves as "the sick man of Asia." But Hacker resists the temptation to engage in a retrospective tourism that would render China into an exotically quaint Other, a spectacle merely meant to amuse or titillate. Instead, he intentionally re-creates a historical landscape that is the very opposite of timeless.

Hacker thus consistently pits paradoxes one against the other, while deep in the background the images of China's great rivers and mountains remind us of the antiquity of a fallen empire and strife-ridden country. The most powerful portion of this book, to me at least, is the chapter that sets turbulence alongside decadence (1919–27), presaging the period of Japan's outright aggression against China (1931–7) before the Pacific War.

The turbulence is manifold. Bandits attack the Blue Express train between Shanghai and Peking in 1923, kidnapping 200 foreigners. Warlords occupy whole regions of the country; and Chang Tso-lin (Zhang Zuolin), the hegemon of Manchuria, stares at the camera's lens in his gaudy gold epaulets, holding a dress sword.

*Left*: This lithograph was copied from a daguerreotype taken by Eliphalet Brown, Jr, who was the official photographer on Commodore Matthew Perry's diplomatic mission to Japan. The daguerreotype was taken when the American fleet of "Black Ships" visited Hong Kong in 1853.

*Right*: This magnificent pair of camels grace the avenue leading to the Ming Tombs. The Scottish photographer John Thomson, who took this photograph in the early 1870s, described these statues as "The finest specimens of sculpture China has to show."

Meanwhile, the Ching (Qing) dynasty is overthrown and we see the last emperor, Pu Yi (Puyi), tutored by Reginald Johnston to ride a bicycle and wear Western eyeglasses, staring shyly out at us as an adolescent in his Manchu robes, and then later with an imperial gaze (oddly undone by the weak eyes behind the very glasses Johnston pressed upon him) wearing the shiny boots, whipcord trousers, and officer's hat of a high-ranking Japanese officer, firmly attached to his samurai sword.

We also sense the insecurity of Shanghai's high-living foreign community, with their White Russian bodyguards, foreign-staffed municipal police force, and Shanghai Volunteers to protect them both against the racketeers of the Green Gang and the "Bolshevik Army" of Chiang Kai-shek sweeping north to wipe out the warlords and imperialists. When he actually arrived outside Shanghai, General Chiang made his peace with the metropolis's native and foreign bankers, crushed the syndicalist strike there by naked force, and turned against his communist allies.

This turnabout opened the way for five years of effervescence on the China coast. While Chiang's Nationalist armies sought to suppress the communist "bandits" in the hinterland, driving Mao and his lieutenants to head north on the Long March, urban life for both Chinese and Westerners took on a new luster. The dazzling lights of Shanghai's Nanking Road reflected what the author styles "the days of no tomorrow." Here, quite graphically, we see the taipans in their dinner jackets, the slim-waisted beauties in high-necked cheongsam dresses slit to the thigh, and the bored dancehall girls who serviced the sailors of a dozen nations who made Shanghai their port of call.

Not all was vice and decadence. The author, using cigarette card drawings and calendar art, also reminds us of the Westernized Chinese élite of this new world of commerce and industry. Pictures of cautiously coquettish young women are posed alongside the ideal mother—no longer the daughter-in-law attached to a large clan, but now the beautifully coiffed wife living alone with her husband and three children in a nuclear family where the kids drink milk, daddy goes off to work as an assistant bank manager, and all hope that they will eventually be able to afford a motorcar for weekend excursions.

The magic garden of modernism withers in 1937 with the Japanese invasion. Arthur Hacker, both textually and graphically, underscores the brutal extent of that conflict. More to the point: he goes beyond that turmoil to foreshadow the communist future ahead, when a peasant based revolution and its leader, Mao Tse-tung (Mao Zedong), will effectively end the turbulence and intentionally extirpate the decadence of those earlier years.

This is a book, therefore, that provides both a panoramic view of China since the sixteenth century and the rapid changes that were to come after 1839. Readers will be swept away by the sense of that timeless landscape, but they will also be borne along by the billows of modern history—its mass movements, civil wars, and revolution—to realize how much travail the country has suffered in the last two centuries, and how many obstacles it has had to overcome to become eventually the power that it is today.

FREDERIC WAKEMAN
Institute of East Asian Studies, University of California

# INTRODUCTION

This book is a collection of images of China that I have gathered at random over a quarter of a century.

Collecting is addictive and the trouble began when I bought a few old postcards of Victorian buildings of Hong Kong that I needed for reference for an historical map of the colony that I was illustrating at the time. One thing led to another and soon everything got completely out of hand ... and I was hooked on collecting.

The compulsive collector is a rather strange creature. He is happy to pay thousands of dollars for a very ugly but extremely rare postage stamp or a piece of Elvis memorabilia. The value of a collectable in monetary terms, be it a Van Gogh or an impaled dead butterfly, is exactly the amount of cash that someone is prepared to pay for it. On the other hand, the artistic and historical value of a picture cannot be calculated in dollars and cents and there is absolutely no way of measuring the emotional value of a particular picture to an individual, be it a magnificent Rembrandt in all its glory or a humble snapshot. People fall in love with images.

My collection expanded rapidly to include images of all kinds: antique photographs, ancient engravings, even lantern slides and the odd scruffy cigarette card. Every image tells a story and the inquisitive and compulsive collector soon drifts into becoming a compulsive reader.

Eventually, my modest collection impelled me into becoming a compulsive writer and it became a working collection. Unlike many historians who, after they have written a book, spend months looking for pictures to illustrate it, I have always done it the other way round and have had a lot of fun finding the story behind an exciting picture.

As most people know very little about Chinese history, I have included a simplified, but I hope not simplistic, introduction of the period covered in every chapter. The history of China, particularly over the last 150 years, is extremely complicated. My aim with these short introductions is to produce an easy-to-read history.

Most Westerners, in particular, know little about China's past. The country has traditionally had a policy of isolationism. In the eighteenth and nineteenth centuries, there were a number of attempts by the West to open dialogs with the Chinese empire. They seldom came to anything because the gulf between the two civilizations was so vast that any discussion was, for both sides, rather like trying to talk to creatures from outer space. It took a war to establish diplomatic relations.

For centuries the emperors of China had regarded diplomacy with foreign countries to be unnecessary because they believed that China was the ultimate power and, like the sun, the rest of the world revolved around it. They had also convinced themselves that all other states were inferior foreign satellites. This is the reason why China is called the Middle Kingdom by the Chinese. Eventually, it dawned on some of the mandarins who became familiar with the West that some of these outer barbarian nations were actually far more powerful and technically more advanced than their own civilization.

These unhappy few kept this knowledge to themselves and dared not tell the emperor. It would have been interpreted as treason and would not have been believed anyway.

The main part of this book tells the story of the century between the signing of the Treaty of Nanking (Nanjing)

*Page 10:* Fantastic images of China were common in the nineteenth century. This engraving of Peking (Beijing) is typical of the period. It was created by a French artist with a vivid imagination. The city wall looks more medieval French than Chinese.

*Page 11:* This picture of a mandarin and his son was taken by the American photographer Milton M. Miller. The pioneer of portraiture in China, Miller is famous for his sensitive portraits of Chinese notables and their families. He worked in Canton between 1861 and 1864.

*Top:* The Armistice Parade in the Forbidden City, Peking, that marked the allied victory over the Germans in World War I. China hoped to regain the German concessions in China, but they were handed over by her wartime allies to Japan.

*Above:* A Chinese soldier at Chusan drawn on the spot by William Alexander in 1793. The soldier's matchlock musket has a forked rest attached to the muzzle. This image was copied frequently by European artists over the next two centuries.

in 1842 after the Opium War and the Japanese attack on Pearl Harbor in 1941. It was a period when China was forced to accept foreign residents through the establishment of treaty ports. It was also the age of the expatriate in China. This book is mainly about these strange creatures: who they were, what they thought, what they did and a few odds and ends about their lifestyle. It is an anecdotal history. Expatriates have always behaved rather differently abroad than they do in their home countries. They are basically a race apart caught in a state of limbo between their native and adopted countries. There are people who even suggest that expatriates should be classified as a nation on their own, particularly with those who have lived most of their life abroad.

This is not one of your hundred-best-pictures type of book which tend to publish the same or similar images. Although I have included a handful of pictures that are well known, particularly in the first chapter, the majority of the images come from a variety of unfamiliar sources: family albums, old magazines, antiquarian books, postcards, lantern slides, posters, cigarette cards, together with hundreds of loose photographs and prints picked up in antique shops and flea markets throughout the world. Some of them cost a small fortune while others were incredibly cheap. The technical quality of the pictures varies enormously, but to me it is the image that is of primary importance rather than the technical skill of the photographer.

The earliest European reproductions of China were engravings and were often rather crudely executed. They were frequently taken from sketches done on the spot by enthusiastic but unskilled amateur artists. They were then engraved in England, France or Holland by craftsmen who were often artists in their own right. Like all true artists, they had a natural creative streak in their makeup and their fertile imaginations frequently came into play. As they had very little source material to go on, they fell back on what is today known as the "borrowed image." Take as an example William Alexander's print of a soldier from a drawing he made in Chusan (Zhoushan) in 1793. It was copied over and over again and appears in dozens of engravings of China throughout the following century, and can even be recognized as a source in the odd modern illustration. It is a striking image.

During the Arrow War (1856–60) the *Illustrated London News* magazine sent professional war artists to China. Their original drawings were usually fairly accurate, but it was of course impossible for an artist working in China to supervise an engraver in Europe. At the same time, the first war photographer in China, Felix Beato, arrived on the scene. By the 1870s there were a number of fine commercial photographers and enthusiastic amateurs taking pictures in China.

Most of the early Victorian pioneers used the collodion wet-plate process to make their negatives, whereby a glass plate had to be prepared and developed on the spot. They used lightproof tents as dark rooms when developing pictures taken out of doors. Long exposures were required and head clamps and other strange devices were used to prevent the subjects from moving. It is therefore not surprising that in many of these early photographs people appear rather static for obvious reasons.

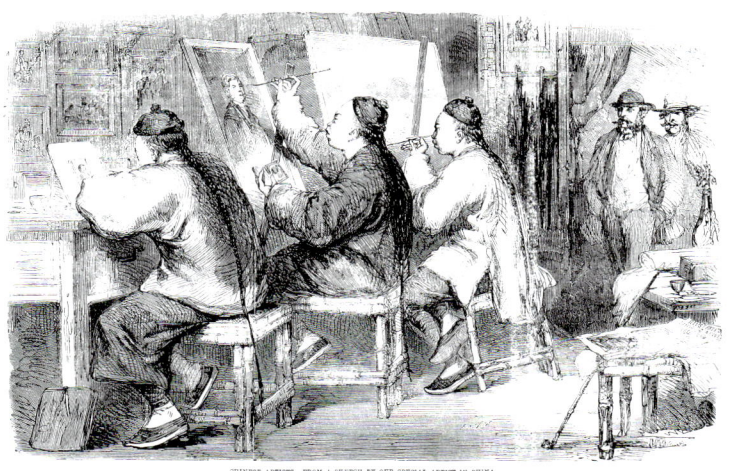

Chinese artists tended to work in teams. A number of artists would often work on the same picture. There were specialists for skies, landscapes, buildings, ships and figures. This is a typical *Illustrated London News* wood engraving. It was published in 1859.

Ma Yue was a wealthy Cantonese comprador working for a British firm. His older principal wife is standing next to him and his second wife is seen here holding her child. The children's amah is the only female in the picture without bound feet.

In the early 1870s, the gelatine dry-plate was invented. It changed everything. The exposure time decreased dramatically. This new technology enabled ordinary people to take pictures with hand-held cameras using ready-sensitized glass plates that could be developed at leisure. With the invention of roll film by George Eastman in 1888, and the production of his first Kodak camera, the age of modern photography began.

Photographers liked to think of themselves as artists, and the first pictures reflected the style of Victorian painting. In the early twentieth century, the influence of French Impressionism is evident. Between the world wars many of the greatest photographers experimented with soft focus. Their work is loved by many collectors, whereas others prefer the pictures by the less fashionable photographers of the period whose images were actually in focus. In the present age of auto-focus and auto-exposure, it is interesting to note how technology is changing the art of photography. Nowadays, the chances of an amateur taking a good picture are far greater than they were in the first half of the twentieth century. Photography was much harder in the old days. Many of the pictures in this volume were taken by gifted amateurs. There is the odd lucky snapshot as well.

A number of "soot and whitewash" news pictures that were taken in the 1930s are also included. These were originally processed in a way designed to produce stark high-contrast black and white prints, because the newspapers of the day were printed on buff-coloured newsprint and the printing was so crude that the black ink that was used generally came out a dirty grey. Consequently, dramatic high-contrast prints were essential. There are many magazine picture editors who today still use pictures of this kind. They also choose to use blurred action pictures because a bit of a blur gives the impression of speed and drama. It adds a bit of excitement to the image.

There are two rival schools of thought when it comes to producing books of old photographs. There is the "warts and all school" who believe that every blemish on the original print should remain, and the other lot who are convinced that every old photograph should be retouched to make it look like new. My sympathies lie with the warts and all faction, because I adore that rich patina of age that tends to enhance the mood of the image. However, this is not true in every case. A faded or badly damaged photograph can benefit enormously from a little judicious retouching, and the unusable image can be made usable. Pictures copied from old magazines often need a bit of work on them, but it is more a question of resurrecting images where there are probably no originals left in existence, rather than restoring them. The secret is to avoid overdoing the retouching or restoring of an old photograph and to make only the minimal changes that are necessary to improve the image. Overworking can destroy the mood and charm of an old picture.

In the past few years, technology has advanced at a bewildering speed. It has created a new art form which is a combination of photography and computer art. It is easy for the art of creating an original image to get buried under a mass of gimmickry. However, there is no substitute for a wonderful and dynamic image which is the rock on which all visual art is built.

*Left*: Japanese Bluejackets in action during the Shanghai War when the Japanese attacked the Chinese municipality of the city in 1932. In this typical "soot and whitewash" war photograph, the drama is increased by the strong contrast of the image.

*Below*: Heinz von Perckhammer's soft focus study of a herd of sheep could easily have been inspired by James McNeill Whistler's famous painting of Old Battersea Bridge. The influence that the work of great artists had on photography was considerable.

INTRODUCTION 15

# Chapter 1

# EAST IS EAST AND WEST IS WEST
## (1557–1860)

Foreign merchants have traded with China since the Tang dynasty (AD 618–907). These early traders were mainly Persians, Arabs and Nestorian Christians. In 1275, Marco Polo, a Venetian merchant, traveled to China. Twenty years later, while in prison in Genoa, he dictated his book, *The Travels of Marco Polo*, to a fellow prisoner. He told of a vast country of enormous wealth ruled by a benign emperor called Kublai Khan. Marco Polo's fabulous Cathay was embellished by his ghostwriter, Rustichello of Pisa; but unlike Sir Walter Raleigh's El Dorado, Cathay actually existed, and two centuries later the first Portuguese ships arrived on the coast of southern China.

The Borgia Pope, Alexander VI, who was Spanish, had divided the unexplored world in two at the Treaty of Tordesillas in 1494. The Spanish were granted most of the Americas, and the Portuguese were given Africa and Asia. Nobody else got a thing.

The Chinese allowed the Portuguese to establish a small fortified trading post at Macau in 1557. Over the next 150 years, the Protestant seafaring nations, the Dutch and the English, systematically conquered most of the Portuguese territory east of Suez and eventually, in 1699, the Chinese allowed the East India Companies of these two countries and those of other nations trading rights at Canton (Guangzhou). For almost two centuries, it was the only Chinese port open to European trade.

China was a vast feudal society ruled by an all-powerful emperor. He called himself the Son of Heaven, and was treated like a god. When the last Ming emperor, Chung Chen (Chongzhen), lost the Mandate of Heaven and hanged himself on a locust tree, the Manchus, a tribe of wild horsemen from north of the Great Wall of China, seized the reins of power. They established the Ching (Qing) dynasty in 1644.

The Manchus were a warrior race, 10 million strong. They were able to control their 400 million Chinese subjects for almost three centuries. They forced the Chinese to adopt the distinctive Manchu hairstyle, the queue, a long plait of hair that hung down the back, as a token of subjection. They were prohibited from taking a Chinese wife or concubine and their women did not bind their feet. The Manchus were a foreign military dictatorship that was supported by an élitist Chinese mandarinate of civil servants, who helped administer the country through an established traditional feudal system that had existed in China for over a thousand years.

The Ching emperors had complete control of the Imperial Army. Every male Manchu was a soldier. The other fighting troops were mainly Mongols. In times of national crisis, Chinese auxiliaries were recruited, but they were disbanded and disarmed once the crisis was over. Every major metropolis had a Tartar City within its walls, where the Manchus and their garrison lived. The Tartar troops were called bannermen and were spread very thinly over the vast countryside of China. When compared to any European army of the period, China's army was mediaeval and was commanded by generals whose tactics were based on Sun Tzu's classic, *The Art of War*, which had been written 750 years before the invention of gunpowder.

During the Opium War (1840–2), the British were fortunate with their military commanders. Sir Hugh

*Previous page*: A family group of Chinese women by the great American photographer Milton M. Miller. He used the collodion wet-plate process which was invented by Frederick Scott Archer in 1851. The original was printed in monochrome and later colored by hand.

*Above*: The Emperor Shun Chih (Shunzhi), the first Manchu emperor of China, who founded the Ching dynasty in 1644. The Manchus were a wild race of horsemen from Manchuria and were looked upon as a foreign dynasty by the Han Chinese.

*Above right*: The missionaries called these warriors "The Tigers of War" for obvious reasons. The spectacular uniform was "supposed to possess the power of petrifying the beholder", but in practice it failed to strike fear into the hearts of Queen Victoria's soldiers.

*Right*: An archer in full dress uniform. Every Manchu was required to be a trained soldier. During the Ching dynasty, many cities had a Tartar quarter where a regular garrison was stationed and where the Manchus lived separately from the indigenous Chinese.

*Opposite*: Before the attack on Chapoo, near Ningpo, in 1842, the overwhelming firepower of the Royal Navy had been deliberately concealed from the emperor. The British fleet blockaded the Grand Canal, cutting off trade between southern China and Peking.

Gough was a Peninsular War veteran, who later won three difficult wars in India. One of his brigade commanders, Lord Saltoun, had led the charge that put Napoleon's Old Guard to flight at the Battle of Waterloo. By comparison, the Chinese general at Canton, Yang Fang, who had put down a Muslim rebellion over a decade earlier, was very old and so deaf that his subordinates could communicate with him only in writing. The Chinese attack on Ningpo (Ningbo) was lead by I-ching, a nephew of the emperor, whose only military experience was as a junior Manchu officer during the suppression of a Muslim uprising. He was a hopeless general and sent his vanguard of sharpshooters, without their firearms, through the west gate of the city, which had been left open deliberately by the British and was mined. Those who were not blown up were shot down in the narrow streets by the British infantry from the windows of the houses. Gough had used a similar tactic to defeat a formidable French army at the siege of Tarifa, thirty years earlier. I-ching's plan was devised with the help of numerology to the extent that he attacked the city on the auspicious hour of the tiger, on the day of the tiger, on the month of the tiger, in the year of the tiger. It was not surprising that the British knew the exact date and time of the attack.

I-ching's troops had little chance against the disciplined musket fire of the British army which had perfected its skills against the mighty forces of Napoleon.

The Chinese had no national navy. Their war junks were incredibly slow and unwieldy and had little firepower. The British secret weapon was the East India Company's iron paddle steamers, like the *Nemesis*, which could maneuver backward and forward at 6 knots and was armed with two 32-pounder pivot guns, 15 swivel guns and a rocket tube. Their fleet of over 50 ships contained three of the Royal Navy's 74-gun men-of-war which had the firepower to breach the walls of any coastal city in China.

China called itself the Middle Kingdom and for thousands of years conducted a policy of aggressive isolationism. Chinese citizens were forbidden to travel abroad. The information of the outside world that filtered up to the emperor was very little, and if accurate, was seldom believed. The Europeans were equally ignorant about China because it was a closed country. They made a number of attempts to establish diplomatic relations with the emperor. Some foreign embassies, like Lord Macartney's in 1793, were treated with exquisite politeness while others, like Lord Amherst's in 1816, were grossly insulted.

Emperor Chien Lung (Qianlong) (1736–95) made his position quite clear in an edict that he sent to King George III in 1793. He pronounced that all barbarian countries were vassal states of the Chinese empire and no foreign legations would be permitted to be established in Peking (Beijing). Furthermore, the king of England, as a vassal of the emperor, should "tremblingly obey" the edict of the Son of Heaven. China's position was not modified until after it lost the Opium War.

The total inability of any European country to communicate directly with the emperor or any Chinese official meant that a problem, however trivial, festered and could not be sorted out by direct diplomatic means. When the English East India Company lost its monopoly, their chief merchant informed the guild of Co-hong merchants in Canton, in the form of a petition, which was passed on through a succession of mandarins, governors, viceroys and chief secretaries until eventually it reached the emperor who was not particularly interested anyway.

The emperor and his advisers had little knowledge of the outside world and assumed that every monarch within his own kingdom had absolute power. China was a feudal state where the concept of democracy was not understood, nor would it have been believed that such an uncivilized form of government could flourish even among remote barbarian nations.

The problem of communication was not confined to the Chinese. For example, a letter sent by a British official from China to the British government could sometimes take eight months to reach its destination. Letters were frequently lost during the voyage to Europe and many were considered not worthy of an instant reply. Between the loss of the East India Company's monopoly on the China trade in 1834 and the Convention of Peking in 1860, Britain had twelve different administrations and fought as many wars, including the Indian Mutiny and the Crimean War. In parliament, it was an age of factionalism, political chaos and enlightened reform and China was nowhere near the top of the agenda of any prime minister.

Both British Tory and Whig prime ministers, Sir Robert Peel and Lord Derby, were against the China wars, but when they came to power, there was nothing they could do about the opium trade because their administrations were too short. The Americans belatedly brought in a law in 1858 that banned their nationals from trading in opium, but it proved difficult to enforce. There was also a strong anti-opium lobby in Britain at the time, but it still took a hundred years for the drug to be banned in the colony of Hong Kong. Although opium, in the form of laudanum, was a problem in the West, it was seldom smoked as in China, and addiction rates were comparatively small.

At some stage it was inevitable that a war would break out between the Chinese empire and some powerful Western nation. If it had not been the British, it would probably have been the French or the Dutch. It was an age when the European powers declared war on each other over what appears today to be mere trivialities. Fortunately, many more conflicts were prevented by diplomacy. Whether diplomacy between China and Britain could have prevented the Opium War is debatable, but at least it would have given peace a chance. Between the Convention of Peking in 1860 and the Boxer Rebellion in 1900, there was peace between Britain and China and they were allies in two world wars. Apart from the Korean War, where the British forces supported the United Nations, there has been peace ever since. This was largely due to diplomacy. As Sir Winston Churchill said in his twilight years, "Jaw-jaw is always better than war."

*Opposite*: A Chinese woodblock illustration from Sun Tzu's *The Art of War*. This Chinese classic on strategy was not much help against a ferocious Irish general who went straight for the jugular and was backed up by the Royal Navy with a fleet of fifty-odd warships.

*Above*: A Chinese drawing of the *Nemesis*. She was the first iron ship to round the Cape of Good Hope. The paddle steamer was the prototype for early Victorian gunboats. She was known as the "Nevermiss" by the British and the "Fire Devil" by the Chinese.

*Left*: A Chinese war junk. These slow-moving, elegant sailing ships were armed with muzzle-loading cannons. The British gunboats carried 32-pound guns and their steamers could be maneuvered at a speed of 8 knots in both directions.

# Foreign Devils from the West

Three centuries after Marco Polo, Portuguese ships sailed into Chinese waters from Malacca, on the southwest coast of the Malay Peninsula, where they had established a colony. Simao d'Andrāde built a fort at Tuen Mun in what is now Hong Kong. He behaved like a pirate and was attacked and defeated by Chinese forces. It was an inauspicious beginning.

Twenty years later, trade developed between the two countries when an annual trade fair was established illegally on a remote island called Shangchuan. St Francis Xavier died there. Japanese pirates known as *wako*, or "sea dwarfs," had plundered the Chinese coast for generations, but they proved no match for the cannons of the Portuguese carracks, which blew them out of the water. As a reward, the Chinese allowed the Portuguese to build an enclave in Macau, in 1557.

The Ming emperors, who had forbidden the Chinese to trade with foreigners, classified Portugal as a suzerain state. This enabled Macau to act as a middleman between China and Japan. They sold silks to the Japanese for silver at an enormous profit. The Spanish tried to set up a rival enclave called El Pinal ("the pine tree"). Romantic historians claim that it was located in Hong Kong, but all trace of it has vanished.

Captain John Weddell arrived with a small British fleet in 1637. He attempted to deliver a letter from King Charles I directly to "the authorities" at Canton. The Chinese answer was to attack the British fleet with fireboats. Weddell sacked a few villages in retaliation. His fleet was sunk on the voyage home.

The Chinese blamed the Portuguese and imposed an enormous fine. Macau could not pay the fine and was banned from trading at Canton. Two years later, all Christians were expelled from Japan. The Dutch had captured Malacca and cut off the sea route to Europe. The golden age of Macau was over.

Entitled *Sketch of the Typa and Macao*, this map was produced around 1775. Two bridges now connect Macau to Taipa. Today Taipa even has an airport, and through reclamation is linked to another island called Coloane to the south.

*Above*: The Praia Grande, Macau, ca. 1843. This engraving was made by Thomas Allom from a sketch by Lieutenant White of the Royal Marines. Recently, this magnificent bay has been transformed into a lake which is dominated by a modern cybernetic fountain.

*Left*: The A-Ma Temple is the oldest building in Macau. The Portuguese pronounced it Amacao or Macao. The temple is dedicated to Ama, the Chinese goddess of sailors and navigators. The lithograph is by the American artist William Heine, who was the official artist on Commodore Matthew Perry's expedition to the China Seas and Japan in 1853.

*Opposite above*: A view of Macau looking north from Penha Hill. The lithograph was made from a drawing by William Heine.

*Opposite below*: The Grotto of Camões. It was here that Portugal's greatest poet, Luis de Camões, wrote his masterpiece *Os Lusiadas*. He held the post of Custodian for the Property of the Dead and Absent when the Portuguese first came to Macau.

*Right*: The ruined facade is all that is left of the Church of St. Paul. It was designed by the Jesuits and built by Chinese and Japanese Christians. The Jesuits were expelled from Macau in 1762. The main body of the church was destroyed in a fire in 1835.

The great Jesuit missionary St Francis Xavier was sent to the Far East in 1549. After converting thousands to Christianity in Goa and Japan, he went on to China where he died a few days after his arrival in 1552.

EAST IS EAST AND WEST IS WEST

*Opposite*: William Alexander's study of a tradesman is taken from his book, *The Costume of China*, which he published in 1805. He notes that in the tradesman's right hand "is a basket of birds' nests, which he carries for sale to the epicures of China."

*Right*: The Frontier Gate between Macau and mainland China is a triumphal arch, erected in 1870 by the Portuguese to celebrate the capture of the Chinese fort of Pak Shan Lan by Lieutenant Vicente Nicolau de Mesquita, twenty years earlier.

*Below*: This chromolithograph of a temporary Chinese opera house constructed from bamboo and mats is titled *Macao. Theater Sing Song*. It was made by the German artist Edward Hildebrandt. Matshed opera houses can still be found in rural China.

EAST IS EAST AND WEST IS WEST

# Matteo Ricci and the First Jesuits in China

The Jesuits were very active in Macau. With the aid of Japanese Christian refugees they built the magnificent Church of St Paul, whose ruined facade is the city's most memorable sight.

Matteo Ricci arrived in Macau in 1582. The young Jesuit's mission was to convert the emperor of China to Christianity. The emperor was known as the Son of Heaven by the Chinese. Consequently, the prospects of persuading him to worship a rival Son of God were very slight.

Ricci was an extremely pragmatic man. Ancestor worship and Confucianism were entrenched among the Chinese. By the free interpretation of the Fifth Commandment (Honor thy Father and thy Mother) and by identifying Confucianism as a code of conduct rather than a religion, he was able to make a few converts.

This extraordinary man mastered Chinese to the extent that he was accepted as a member of the literati. In 1600, on a visit to the Board of Mathematics, he was shown a celestial sphere that had been constructed by Kuo Shou-ching (Guo Shoujing) in the Yuan dynasty. It had been designed to be used at Linfen in Shansi (Shanxi). It was later moved to Nanking (Nanjing), which was on a different latitude, and as a consequence it became inaccurate. After Ricci's death, another Jesuit, Ferdinand Verbiest, constructed a new set of astronomical instruments, some of which can be seen today in the ancient Peking observatory together with Kuo's equatorial torquetum. Verbiest and his colleague, Adam Schall, were appointed by Emperor Kang Hsi (Kangxi) to correct the Chinese calendar.

The Jesuits were also involved in designing the Summer Palace (Yuanmingyuan). They contributed a great deal to the culture and sciences of China and helped revive many of China's ancient skills that had been lost over the ages. After Kang Hsi asked the Pope to supply him with one of his nieces as a concubine and got no reply from His Holiness, the Jesuits lost the emperor's trust.

*Right*: This armillary sphere, constructed by Kuo Shou-ching in the Yuan dynasty, was one of the astronomical instruments seen by the Jesuit, Matteo Ricci, on his visit to the Board of Mathematics. His skill at astronomy provided him with an entrée to the imperial court.

*Opposite*: The Jesuit Matteo Ricci, seen here on the left, in his chapel at Peking. He is dressed in the costume of the Chinese literati. Despite spending twelve years in Peking, he never actually succeeded in obtaining an interview with the emperor.

*Above*: The Emperor Kang Hsi (Kangxi) paying a visit to the Jesuit church in Peking. He commissioned Ferdinand Verbiest to correct the imperial calendar. Kang Hsi, while respecting the Jesuits' technical abilities, kept a wary eye on their activities.

*Right*: The Peking observatory, as it looked in 1934. It still stands on a remnant of the ancient east wall of the Tartar City, near the railway station. It has on display some of the original astronomical instruments designed by the Jesuits.

# The John Company and Others

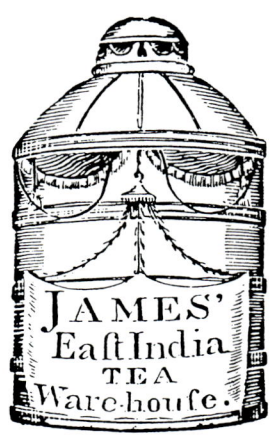

"I have singed the King of Spain's beard," declared Sir Francis Drake, after his fleet had burned twenty-four ships in Cadiz harbor in 1587. On his return journey to England, he captured the *San Felipe*, a Portuguese carrack, returning from the East Indies. Her cargo of silk, spices and jewels was worth three times as much as the shipping Drake had destroyed in Cadiz. This inspired the English and Dutch to send expeditions to the Far East in search of trade and plunder.

Queen Elizabeth granted a charter to the merchants of London to trade in the Spice Islands (Indonesia). They formed the Honourable East India Company, nicknamed the John Company. The first fleet sailed east in 1601.

In 1648, the Chinese Emperor Kang Hsi decided to allow limited trade with foreigners of all nations and the John Company established a trading factory at Canton. At that time, the Dutch East India Company was the dominant European power in the Spice Islands, whereas the John Company was firmly established in Bombay, Madras and Calcutta.

There were other East India Companies: French, Spanish, Danish and Swedish. These European monopolies were allowed only to trade with a guild of Chinese merchants known as the Co-hong who were controlled by a customs official called the Hoppo.

Foreign merchants were confined to a small area of Canton and allowed to live there only for a few months every year. Trade could be conducted only by fawning to the mandarins and paying them enormous bribes. The East India companies were monopolies; they made fantastic profits, and the directors in London, Amsterdam and Paris did not object too loudly if their staff in a remote city in China had to grovel to the mandarins and pay a certain amount of bribe money, provided that it oiled the wheels of commerce. This period was called the golden age of China trade. I can't think why.

*Left*: These delightful vignettes are the work of Thomas Bewick, who was the father of the wood engraving. The technique that he developed in England in the eighteenth century was also known as "white line engraving" and is still used by illustrators today.

*Below*: The busy port of Canton. The merchant ships of the great European East India Companies at anchor surrounded by Chinese junks and sampans. This seventeenth century engraving was made by the Dutch artist John Nievhoff.

EAST IS EAST AND WEST IS WEST

*Above*: A street in Canton in the early nineteenth century. In 1685, the Emperor Kang Hsi allowed limited trade with foreigners at Canton. The principal imports of the East India Company, nicknamed the John Company, were tea, silk and porcelain which they bought with silver.

*Above right*: The crest of Britain's Honourable East India Company depicts the third company headquarters in Leadenhall Street, London. It was used between 1648 and 1726. The building had been owned formerly by Lord Craven, the Lord Mayor of London.

*Above*: Sir Thomas Smythe, the founder of the Honourable East India Company. Four of the company's ships made the first voyage to Sumatra in 1601. They returned to England in 1603 with a cargo of pepper and other spices.

EAST IS EAST AND WEST IS WEST 35

*Below*: A social gathering in a mandarin's palace. In the background are two jugglers accompanied by a drummer. Jugglers, contortionists, acrobats, conjurors and martial arts experts have always provided a popular form of entertainment in China.

*Right*: An allegorical engraving of Anglo-Chinese trade in the eighteenth century. The three great Chinese commodities of silk, tea and porcelain can be seen behind the Chinese merchant. The nature of the goods that the British merchant is selling is tactfully concealed.

*Below right*: East India House in 1815. This massive neoclassical building was a symbol of the wealth of the John Company at the height of its financial power. The Indian Mutiny sealed the fate of the company, and the house was demolished in 1861.

EAST IS EAST AND WEST IS WEST

# The Swedish East India Company

The John Company and the Dutch East India Company were vast commercial empires with their own private armies and navies. These predatory conglomerates frequently declared war on hapless Asian states without consulting their national governments.

The Dutch company employed 20,000 men and owned 200 ships. By contrast, the Swedish company seldom sent more than three ships a year to China. It was founded by a Swedish merchant, Nicholas Sahlgren, and a Scotsman, Colin Campbell, who had been expelled from the John Company in the aftermath of the South Sea Bubble financial scandal that rocked London in 1728.

Campbell was appointed chief supercargo. His ship, *Friedericus Rex*, arrived at Whampoa (Whampo) on 7 September 1732, six months after leaving Sweden. He had to pay a customs tax to the Hoppo in order to trade, most of which went into the Hoppo's pocket. This official was arrested for corruption and Campbell had to pay even more money to the new Hoppo, who in turn was replaced.

The interpreters who conducted the business were supplied by the Co-hong Chinese merchants. Campbell was assigned "a villain of a linguist," who tried to involve the Scot in a scam to swindle the Swedish company, which in reality meant robbing himself, as a director.

"As to the Dutch Super Cargos," wrote Campbell in his diary, "there never were such a set of knaves and fools." He had a legitimate complaint. The Dutch delayed his ship at Batavia (Jakarta) on the return journey.

Swedish trade was a simple three-way affair. Their ships sold timber and iron to Spain for silver. This paid for Chinese tea, silks and porcelain. The profit came mainly from tea that was sold by auction in Sweden. After the auction, all the accounts were destroyed because most of the tea was then smuggled illegally into Britain. When the British Whig parliament reduced the tax on tea in 1784, it was the beginning of the end for the Swedish company.

*Above*: Colin Campbell was one of the founders of the Swedish East India Company. He was the leading merchant on the company's first voyage to China. His diary is a record of the perilous voyage and the problems faced by European traders.

*Opposite below*: This late eighteenth century painting shows the Swedish flag flying in front of the foreign factories at Canton. Today, the area where the factories stood before they were burnt down during the Arrow War, is called Shisanhanglu.

*Right*: A Swedish East Indiamen outside Nya Elfsborg, Gothenburg. Between Campbell's first voyage in the *Friedericus Rex* in 1732 and the final voyage of the *Maria Carolina* in 1804, the Swedish East India Company made over a hundred expeditions to China.

*Below*: The Swedish East India Company's coat of arms.

*Left*: Tea time in China. This wood engraving is typical of the illustrations that decorated books on China during the Victorian age.

*Below*: The culture and preparation of tea. The Swedish East India Company's main profits came from tea, most of which was smuggled into England. The company managed to survive for another twenty years after the British government reduced the tax on tea.

*Above*: The fountain court of Conseequa's house near Canton. Co-hong merchants, although frequently pleading poverty, lived in splendor in vast mansions. This engraving was based on a drawing owned by Sir George Staunton.

*Left*: Dyeing and winding silk. Campbell's departure from China was delayed by fourteen days because "Pinky," a Co-hong merchant, failed to honor his contract without extra payment. Campbell refused to be blackmailed and bought some more tea instead from a rival trader.

# The Embassies That Failed

Portugal, Holland and Russia had all tried to establish diplomatic relations with China and failed. In 1792, Britain sent Lord Macartney to China principally to attempt to establish an embassy in Peking with the Emperor Chien Lung (Qianlong).

It was important to the British government that Chien Lung should treat King George III as an equal. Macartney's problems began when the boat taking him by river to Peking displayed a banner which read "Tribute-embassy from Red Barbarians."

Macartney had been instructed to do "nothing derogatory to dignity." If he kowtowed to the emperor and was seen to grovel before the Dragon Throne, it would be interpreted that King George acknowledged being a cringing subject of the emperor of China. The Chinese mandarins did everything they could to persuade him to kowtow. Macartney suggested that he might comply, but only if a mandarin of a similar rank kowtowed before a portrait of King George. This compromise proved unacceptable.

Macartney decided to send a letter directly to Chien Lung. It had to be written in an elaborate court style in order to be acceptable. He persuaded a Chinese to compose a letter secretly on condition that George Staunton, his secretary's son, would write a fair copy in Chinese. George had learnt to write Chinese on the voyage out. He was only twelve years old.

To everyone's amazement, Chien Lung allowed Macartney an audience without performing the kowtow. I have seen "King Solomon in all his Glory," wrote Macartney afterwards, in his diary.

Even though the mission failed, the Chinese authorities were exquisitely polite to Macartney. By contrast, in 1816 their treatment of Lord Amherst's embassy seemed to be specifically designed to humiliate the British.

The Emperor Chia Ching (Jianqing) in a letter to the British king wrote: "If you loyally accept OUR sovereignty there is really no need for these stated appearances to prove that you are indeed OUR vassal." It was written the year after Britain had won the Battle of Waterloo.

**Lord Macartney had a fine diplomatic record when he was selected to lead the embassy to China. His term as British Envoy Extraordinary to the Court of Catherine the Great of Russia had been a brilliant success. She gave him a snuffbox.**

*Left*: The Emperor Chien Lung arrives in his palanquin at his *yurt* in Jehol (Chengde) to give audience to Lord Macartney in September 1793. Macartney and his interpreter, 12-year-old George Staunton, can be seen on the right of the picture.

*Below*: The Stone Boat was in the compound used by the embassy in Peking. The artist William Alexander wrote that "the upper part of this whimsical building was used by part of the suite of the Embassy as a dining room."

EAST IS EAST AND WEST IS WEST

# An Artist on the Grand Canal

On the return journey, Macartney's embassy traveled most of the way by boat to Canton via the Grand Canal, parts of which date back to 486 BC to the Wu dynasty. Marco Polo's patron, the Mongol emperor Kublai Khan, extended it so that he could ship grain from the Yangtze River to feed the population of his new capital, Dadu (Peking). It was frequently in a state of disrepair. It is the longest and oldest canal in the world.

In Macartney's entourage was an architectural draftsman called William Alexander. The convoy moved at a leisurely pace and Alexander was able to record the scenery and people of the passing countryside. It was before the age of steam and Britain was in the process of building its own canal network.

Alexander was fascinated by Chinese engineering, the sail-driven wheelbarrows, the chain-pumps and the way they dragged their flat-bottomed barges over ramps from one level to the other. However, almost everything in China was done by hand. He loved drawing ships. When there was no wind, the canal craft were towed by a multitude of coolies known as "trackers."

"These are kept in full exertion by a task-master, who most liberally applies a whip, where he sees a disposition to idleness," wrote Alexander. "The chief food of these poor labourers is rice; and they consider it a luxury, when they can procure vegetables fried in rancid oil, or animal offal, to mix with it."

By contrast, members of the embassy enjoyed exotic banquets. "The entertainment," he wrote, "consisted of a profusion of poultry, confectionery, fresh fruits, preserves, jars of wine, &c. &c." Military garrisons turned out and fired salutes in their honor. He noted that "The Chinese on these occasions never use more than three guns, which are always fired perpendicular, to prevent accidents."

It was all show. The emperor's edict, which refused any concessions to the British, had actually been written three days before Macartney landed and before any negotiations had actually begun.

A sail-driven cart. This phenomenon was well known in the West. Over a century before William Alexander went to China, John Milton wrote in his epic poem, *Paradise Lost*, that the "Chinese drive, with sails and wind, their cany waggons light."

*Left*: Canal coolies were called "trackers." Their job was to pull canal and river barges. The China pony was an unpredictable, volatile creature and was unsuited to the tasks performed by canal horses in Europe. Manpower was cheaper and more reliable.

*Below*: The front view of a boat being dragged up a 40-degree stone slope backwards. Instead of using locks, Chinese canal craft were pulled up stone ramps to higher water beyond by a combination of manpower, ropes, pulleys and capstans.

*Left*: "Watermen, peasantry, and others, employed in the open air," wrote Alexander, "are generally provided with a coat made of straw, from which the rain runs off, as from the feathers of an aquatic bird." Straw raincoats were still around in the twentieth century.

*Right*: The junks that were used to carry the embassy's minor officials and Macartney's gifts for the emperor. They were flat-bottomed craft, drawing little water, and suitable for river travel. Each junk could carry about 200 tons of cargo.

*Below*: Yang-chau (Yangzhou) is on the Grand Canal a few miles north of the Yangtze. Marco Polo is said to have governed the city for three years when he was employed as an official by the Emperor Kublai Khan during the Yuan dynasty.

*Left*: A mandarin's traveling boat. "The double umbrella, or ensign of authority, is conspicuously placed to demand respect." The Chinese characters on the flag at the stern indicated the mandarin's rank, warning other craft to move out of the way.

*Below*: The bridge at Soochow (Suzhou) was decorated in Macartney's honor with a "temporary ornament" of bamboo scaffolding hung with lanterns and silk ribbons. A modest guard of honor composed of six soldiers can be seen on the bridge.

EAST IS EAST AND WEST IS WEST

# The Interlopers and Taipans

There is always some enterprising individual who will find a way round a monopoly. In the case of the John Company's monopoly, the "Country Trade" provided a convenient loophole. It allowed for private commerce to be conducted between India and other ports of Asia, including China and Siam (Thailand).

Silver, the currency of China, had become scarce because of the Napoleonic War and the revolutions in South America. Most Chinese goods had to be paid for in this metal. About the only commodity that could be sold for silver was opium.

The Emperor Yung Cheng (Yongzheng) banned opium smoking in 1729, but neglected to prohibit its import. Consequently, the John Company started growing it in India and selling it legally in China. They stopped selling the drug in China when the Emperor Chia Ching eventually got around to banning its import in 1796.

However, they sold Indian opium to the country traders, or "Interlopers," who smuggled it into China. They paid for the drug with Chinese silver they received for the opium. The Interlopers established a base at Lintin Island in the mouth of the Pearl River, where they sold opium to Chinese smugglers and the corrupt mandarins of the Opium Suppression Force. It was smuggled ashore in fast Chinese longboats known as "scrambling crabs."

The principal Scottish smugglers were William Jardine, James Matheson and James Innes, the unspeakable Laird of Dunkinty. Their rivals were the Englishman Lancelot Dent and the Americans Augustine Heard and Warren Delano Jr. These Interlopers were called taipans.

The Machiavellian Jardine was a former ship's surgeon with the John Company, and his Chinese nickname was "Iron-Headed Old Rat." Innes was a cantankerous thug and Delano was the grandfather of Franklin Delano Roosevelt, the president of the United States of America.

Many of the Interlopers were devout Christians, including Matheson, who was made a baronet for feeding the population of the Isle of Lewis during the Scottish potato famine. He had bought a vast estate there with drug money. He later became the local member of parliament.

*Right*: Opium smokers relaxing over a pipe in a fashionable divan. However, most opium dens were sordid hellholes. Opium smoking was mainly confined to the wealthy upper class before the taipans started importing the drug in vast quantities.

*Opposite*: A popular postcard of an opium smoker. The gentleman in this elegant picture was probably a member of the literati indulging in his favorite vice in the comfort of his own home. Some mansions had special rooms that were used exclusively for smoking.

48   CHINA ILLUSTRATED

*Top*: Dr William Jardine was a ship's surgeon before becoming the principal opium smuggler in China. He advised the British foreign minister, Lord Palmerston, on the strategy that was used by the British forces during the Opium War.

*Above*: James Matheson who, with his fellow Scot, Dr William Jardine, founded Jardine, Matheson & Co. It was known as the "Princely Hong." Matheson published the first foreign newspaper in China, the *Canton Register*. He later became a member of parliament.

*Right*: Lintin Island was a safe haven for opium ships in the Pearl River delta. Fifty or sixty vessels would anchor here during the trading season. They would sell their deadly cargo to Chinese opium dealers who would smuggle it into China in junks and "scrambling crabs."

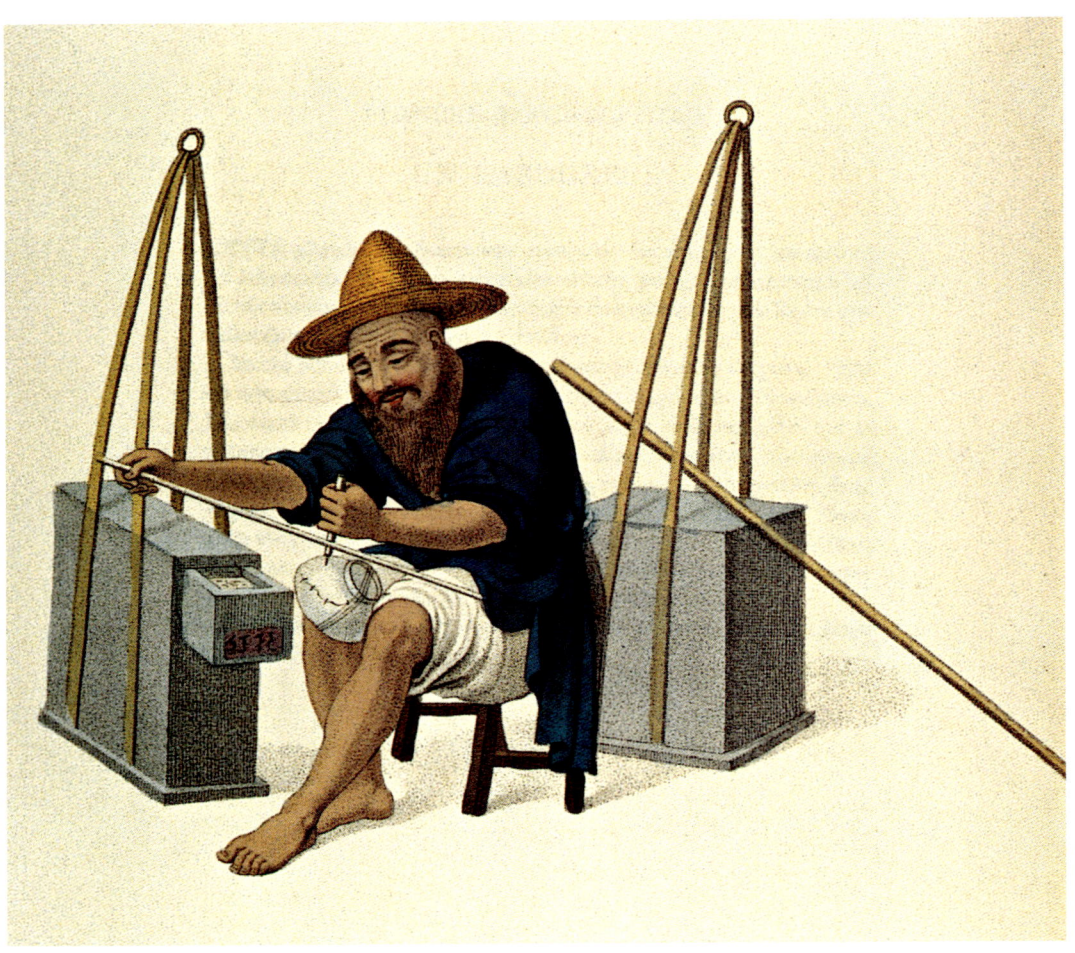

*Above*: A porcelain mender using a small diamond-pointed drill to make holes in a bowl before stitching the pieces together with wire. Porcelain was a major Chinese export to the West. The Europeans did not learn how to manufacture it until the eighteenth century.

*Right*: A moneychanger, or *shroff*, examining a coin. Foreign silver coins became the principal currency in the treaty ports. The most popular coin was the Mexican silver dollar. A moneychanger determined the value of a silver coin by weighing it.

*Opposite*: A woman preparing tea. "The laborious Chinese porter relishes it equally with the most delicate European lady," wrote Major George Henry Mason, who commissioned a Cantonese artist, Pu Qua, to do these drawings which he later published.

# Laboriously Vile

The Honourable East India Company lost its monopoly of trade with China by an Act of Parliament in 1833. The Interlopers were delighted and the Chinese were bewildered. They could not understand why an Outer Barbarian vassal government would want to change the system.

To handle British interests in Canton, the British Foreign Secretary, Lord Palmerston, appointed Lord Napier Chief Superintendent of Trade. The Chinese had expected the British to send a merchant, not an official. Napier arrived in Canton without a permit and demanded to see the viceroy of Kwangtung (Guangdong) province.

The Chinese mandarinate assumed correctly that it was an attempt to establish diplomatic relations through a *fait accompli* and refused even to speak to him. They instructed the Co-hong merchants to persuade Napier to leave, and threatened to ban all trade with foreigners if he refused. Jardine advised Napier to stand firm.

Napier became so frustrated that he posted a proclamation in Chinese libeling the viceroy, who replied by stopping all trade and nailing a notice to the John Company's front door, where he used two Chinese characters to describe Napier, translated as "Laboriously Vile."

Napier ordered two Royal Navy frigates to sail upriver. On the way they fought the Battle of the Bogue, only to become becalmed and then trapped by the Chinese at Whampoa. As a show of force it was a failure.

The strain proved too much for Napier, who was by now a sick man. He applied for a permit to leave Canton and suffered the humiliation of being taken in a Chinese junk under guard to Macau, where he died three days later. The appointment of Napier had proved to be a disaster.

Jardine and his supporters petitioned King William IV to send a strong naval force to China. This request was ignored by the Duke of Wellington who had replaced Palmerston as Foreign Secretary. The Iron Duke disliked *box wallahs* like Jardine, and the new Tory Prime Minister, Sir Robert Peel, a politician with a conscience, loathed the opium trade.

The mandarinate's normal means of communication with foreign traders was through the Co-hong merchants or by posting notices. They were very perturbed when Lord Napier stuck up his own proclamation that libeled the viceroy.

*Above*: The first Battle of the Bogue, 1834. Chinese gunners in the Bogue Forts fired on two Royal Navy frigates, HMS *Andromache* and HMS *Imogene*, which had become becalmed. The British returned fire before sailing upriver to Whampoa.

*Left*: The Canton factories. There were thirteen of them in a terrace extending about 1,000 feet. There was a recreation area between them and the river. Foreign traders were officially allowed to live there only during the trading season.

EAST IS EAST AND WEST IS WEST

Whampoa from Dane's Island. The Chinese trapped the British frigates here by sinking twelve barges loaded with stones to block the channel to Canton. They prepared a hundred fireboats and erected shore batteries bristling with cannon manned by a small army.

# An American at Canton

William Hunter arrived in Canton in 1825. He was twelve years old and was apprenticed to an American opium trader on the condition that he learn Chinese. Teaching a foreigner Chinese carried the death penalty in imperial China, so Hunter was sent to the Anglo-Chinese College at Malacca to study the language.

Competent linguists were rare and everybody else used pidgin English. This multilingual baby talk was easy to learn. There were only about 500 words. It was a simple means of communication that worked. Words like chit, chow, char, cumshaw, josshouse, squeeze and ketchup are still used today with expressions like "can do" and "long time no see." However, smellum-wata (perfume) and cow-oil (butter) have vanished.

In his old age, Hunter wrote The "Fan-Kwae" at Canton Before Treaty Days describing his experiences as an American opium trader. Foreigners, as well as being confined to a small area known as "the factories," were required to obey a number of regulations, most of which they ignored. The mandarins seldom enforced them strictly except in rare times of crisis like "The Napier Fizzle." A factory was not a factory in the modern sense, as nothing was manufactured there. It was basically an office, warehouse and luxurious residential gentlemen's club combined.

There was a regulation which, as the British artist George Chinnery put it, "forbids the softer sex from coming and bothering us here." He was a refugee from Mrs Chinnery who was no beauty. There was consternation in the factories when a bevy of "foreign devil females" arrived on an illicit visit. The mandarins threatened to cut off all trade if they did not leave immediately. Like today's soft-drug lobby, Hunter reasoned, "As compared with the use of spirituous liquors in the United States and England, and the evil consequences of it, that of opium was infinitesimal."

Not everybody agreed. Sir George Staunton, Macartney's former page, stated in Parliament, "If there had been no opium, there had been no war."

*Left*: The Thirteen Factories Street at Canton. This wood engraving is based on a drawing made by Auguste Borget who stayed in the factories for ten months during 1838 and 1839, just before the start of the Opium War.

*Opposite*: A village scene. Most of Borget's paintings and prints of China are riverscapes. At the time, foreigners were confined to the factories, but exploring the vicinity by boat was tolerated by the authorities provided that the *fan-kwaes* behaved themselves.

*Right*: A commercial junk anchored in the Pearl River. Hunter was a founding member of the Canton Regatta Club created "for boat-pulling and sailing on the river." Racing was officially forbidden, an edict that Hunter and his fellow enthusiasts ignored.

*Below*: Cooked food stalls were, and still are, to be found in every city in China. In spite of attempts by generations of officials to clear them from the streets, the Chinese food hawker is alive and well. They are a timeless feature of Chinese urban life.

*Right*: Unloading goods at a foreign factory in Canton. This wood engraving was printed in *La Chine Ouverte* by P. E. Forgues. The book is lavishly illustrated with scores of Borget's engravings. It was published in France in 1845, six years after Borget left China.

*Below*: A salt merchant's house in Canton. There had been a salt monopoly in China since the second century BC. Members of the cartel of salt merchants were extremely wealthy. The monopoly was a frequent cause of unrest in China.

EAST IS EAST AND WEST IS WEST  61

# Commissioner Lin and Captain Elliot

Captain Charles Elliot was a junior member of Lord Napier's staff. The British taipans and Viceroy Teng Ting-chen (Deng Tingzhen), who was involved in the opium trade himself, despised Napier's successors. When they eventually retired, Elliot was left in charge.

The opium problem got completely out of hand, so Emperor Tao Kuang (Daoguang) sent Lin Tse-hsu (Lin Zexu), an incorruptible official, to Canton to eliminate the opium trade. Commissioner Lin arrived in Canton in March 1839. Within a few days he had terrified the viceroy, the Co-hong merchants and the foreign traders. His troops surrounded the factories and cut off all the supplies. Elliot sneaked through the blockade and took control of the situation.

Lin ordered the foreigners to give him all the opium that was stored in their ships. By guaranteeing the taipans that they would be reimbursed by the British government, Elliot persuaded them to surrender 20,283 chests of opium, which Lin destroyed. Elliot's major concern was for the lives of the British subjects held hostage in the factories. They were released, but Lin piled on the pressure and within six months the British population of Macau had sought refuge aboard merchant ships in Hong Kong harbor. Elliot realized its potential as a port.

Two small Royal Navy frigates arrived in the autumn. On 3 November 1839, the British attacked Admiral Kwan's war junks, which threatened the refugee fleet. At the Battle of Chuenpee (Chuanbi), the Chinese junks would have been completely annihilated if Elliot, a compassionate man, had not stopped the slaughter. Captain Henry Smith, the British naval commander, was furious.

A British task force arrived from India in June and sailed up to Chusan (Zhoushan), an island at the mouth of the Yangtze River, where they captured Tinghai after an awesome display of firepower. The emperor was alarmed and appointed Kishen (Qishan) Grand Secretary, to replace Lin. He was ordered to negotiate with Elliot. The result was the Convention of Chuenpee, which ceded Hong Kong Island to the British, in 1841.

Commissioner Lin was sent to Canton to stamp out the opium trade. This incorruptible mandarin had previously had no contact with Outer Barbarians and consequently completely underestimated the firepower of the British forces.

*Far left*: The Emperor Tao Kuang (Daoguang) was completely misinformed by his officials in southern China about the strength of the naval power of the British. The mandarins were afraid to tell him the truth and instead deliberately misled him.

*Left*: During the first phase of the Opium War, Captain Charles Elliot forced the Manchus to cede Hong Kong to the British. Lord Palmerston was unimpressed. He called the island "a barren rock with hardly a house upon it" and dismissed Elliot from his post.

*Below*: This engraving of the capture of Chuenpee, was based on a sketch by Lieutenant White of the Royal Marines. The battle was mainly a naval affair and marked the real beginning of the Opium War. It was fought on 3 November 1839.

EAST IS EAST AND WEST IS WEST

# Two Irishmen

The Opium War continued after the emperor had refused to ratify Kishen's treaty and put a price of $50,000 on Elliot's head. Major-General Sir Hugh Gough arrived from India and took control of the army.

The British navy fought their way up to Canton and Gough's small army surprised the Chinese by capturing the heights above the city. Canton was at the mercy of Gough's artillery and the British fleet. An hour before the attack, Elliot accepted another truce and lost the initiative. The Chinese strategy was based on Sun Tzu's *The Art of War*. He wrote, "The supreme art of war is to subdue the enemy without fighting." If Palmerston had not dismissed Elliot, it might have worked.

It is claimed unfairly that Gough's only tactic was the charge. He liked to "be in at them with the bayonet!" He had fought in almost every battle during the Peninsular War. At Tarifa, with a small force of infantry, he had destroyed a Napoleonic army of 15,000 men and captured the French siege train. As the commander-in-chief of British armies in China and later India, Gough won four wars.

Elliot's replacement, Sir Henry Pottinger, was also a man of action. In his youth he had traveled 2,312 miles through Baluchistan, Afghanistan and Persia as a spy, disguised as a Tartar holy man. To convince a village elder that you are a venerable Tartar hadji, when you have a thick Belfast accent, requires a certain amount of the blarney. Pottinger was only twenty at the time.

Sir Henry had an invincible fleet, a fighting general and a competent admiral. He sailed up the Yangtze and captured Ningpo and blockaded the Grand Canal. This created a serious food problem in Peking. In 1841, he captured Shanghai and his fleet threatened Nanking. There were negotiations and when the Chinese tried to stall, "the barbarian Pottinger only knit his brows, and said 'No!'" The result was the Treaty of Nanking that ceded Hong Kong Island to Britain, opened five ports to foreign trade and established diplomatic relations between the two great nations.

*Far left*: Sir Henry Pottinger replaced Captain Elliot as Plenipotentiary and Superintendent of Trade in China. He forced the Manchus to sign the Treaty of Nanking which brought the Opium War to an end. He was the first governor of Hong Kong.

*Left*: Major-General Sir Hugh Gough was the British army commander-in-chief during the Opium War. Gough had fought in every major battle in the Peninsular War. He was later the victor of both Anglo-Sikh Wars. He never lost a battle.

*Left*: The British captured Ningpo in October 1841 and made it their winter headquarters. The emperor's forces tried to recapture the city and walked into a trap. The British left the west gate open and when the enemy entered the city they were slaughtered.

*Below*: The taking of Chinkiang. The attack was led by Major-General Lord Saltoun's First Brigade. The whole British force was involved. The battle is remembered for the outstanding courage of the Tartar troops and the heavy casualties they inflicted on the British.

The death of Colonel Tomlinson showing British troops using controlled fire. At the Battle of Waterloo, one volley of musketry stopped Napoleon's Old Guard. This was followed by a bayonet charge led by Lord Saltoun. The Old Guard ran away for the first time.

# The Pirates of the South China Sea

China has seldom been a significant sea power. But in 1281, the great Mongol emperor, Kublai Khan, had a fleet strong enough to attempt to invade Japan. A typhoon destroyed his fleet. The Japanese called it a *kamikaze*, which means a divine wind.

During the Ming dynasty, the fleet of the great eunuch admiral Cheng Ho (Zheng He) sailed as far as Africa. The eunuchs, who controlled the Chinese navy, were at loggerheads with Emperor Cheng Tung's (Zhengtong's) Confucian advisers, who persuaded the emperor to disband his navy, leaving China's coastline at the mercy of the Japanese *wako* pirates.

In the last years of the Ming dynasty, a Macau merchant, Nicholas Iquan, turned to piracy. He was bribed to change sides and became an imperial admiral. Then the Manchus invaded China. Iquan attempted to change sides again, but during the negotiations he was murdered. This proved to be a costly mistake, because his son Koxinga (Guoxingye) inherited Iquan's fleet and carried on the fight from Taiwan.

In 1659, Koxinga descended on Nanking with a formidable fleet. On the day before the final assault, he held a birthday party. The Manchus launched a surprise attack and slaughtered over 100,000 drunks. Koxinga escaped to Taiwan.

The Manchus could not defeat him, so they adopted a "scorched earth" policy. They ordered everyone living on the coast to move 17 miles inland on pain of death. Consequently, the fisherfolk became pirates.

The greatest of these was Cheng I-sao (Mrs Cheng). In 1810, she defeated a Manchu fleet of 93 war junks and six Portuguese vessels at Chek Lap Kok, the site of today's Hong Kong International Airport. Mrs Cheng was notoriously promiscuous. Jealousy caused her two principal lieutenants to change sides and they were made Manchu admirals. They persuaded Mrs Cheng to surrender. Hong Kong inherited the pirate problem. The British governor, Sir George Bonham, a successful pirate fighter, and the viceroy of Kwangtung joined forces and to everybody's surprise annihilated the pirates.

Cheng I-sao (Mrs. Cheng) took command of her husband's pirate fleet after his death. She defeated a formidable Manchu fleet at Chek Lap Kok in 1810. Later her lieutenants changed sides and were made admirals. They persuaded her to surrender.

*Left*: Sir George Bonham was a formidable pirate fighter. Before he became governor of Hong Kong in 1848, his "Q Boats" (British warships disguised as Arab traders), had cleared the waters around Singapore, and what is now Malaysia, of pirates.

*Below*: The capture and destruction of thirteen pirate junks in Mirs Bay by HMS *Medea* in 1850. This joint Anglo-Chinese operation was conducted at the request of the Chinese authorities. Captain Lockyer, its commander, was assisted by a mandarin.

CAPTURE AND DESTRUCTION OF THIRTEEN PIRATICAL CHINESE JUNKS, IN MIR'S BAY, BY H. M. STEAMER "MEDEA."

EAST IS EAST AND WEST IS WEST

*Left*: The British man-of-war HMS *Actaeon* rescues a Chinese junk from pirates in the Yellow Sea in 1859. The warship towed the damaged junk to Shanghai. The *Actaeon* was paid $4,000 salvage money which the captain distributed among the crew.

*Below:* The slow-moving, bat-winged junks of the South China Sea were easy prey for swift pirate galleys which did not have to rely on wind power. These craft were also used for opium smuggling and were known as "scrambling crabs."

*Right*: Kublai Khan's Mongol war fleet destroyed the Sung (Song) emperor's navy in 1279, in a ferocious sea battle that lasted for three weeks. The boy emperor, Bing Di, was drowned and Kublai Khan became the first emperor of the Yuan dynasty.

*Below*: Captured pirates aboard an imperial Chinese junk. This wood engraving comes from *La Chine Ouverte* by "Old Nick" and was made by Auguste Borget in 1845, six years after he left China.

KOXINGA

Koxinga was probably the most successful Asian pirate in the history of mankind. He had a pirate fleet of over 3,000 junks and an army of 200,000 men. In 1661, he captured Taiwan from the Dutch.

EAST IS EAST AND WEST IS WEST

The boats of HMS *Cleopatra* destroying a fleet of pirate junks in Bias Bay in 1851. This sea fight was an incident in the successful Anglo-Chinese campaign to annihilate piracy in the South China Sea, that was instigated by Hong Kong governor Sir George Bonham.

# Harry Parkes and the Arrow War

Canton was one of the five original treaty ports where foreigners were allowed to trade. Unlike in Shanghai, there was intense friction between foreigners and the Chinese population and officials. It boiled over when some mandarins boarded a ship called the *Arrow* and arrested the crew whom they suspected of being pirates.

The ship, although Chinese owned, was flying the Union Jack, which it had no right to do. The hot-headed Acting British Consul, Harry Parkes, objected and got a cuff round the ear for his pains. Parkes complained to Sir John Bowring, Governor of Hong Kong, who sent a few gunboats to shell Canton.

In so doing, he had disobeyed a standing instruction from the British government not to use force in any dispute with China, but Palmerston, who was now Prime Minister, decided that it was an act of war. However, parliament did not agree and his administration was defeated in the House of Commons; but the war continued.

Lord Elgin was sent to China to sort out the matter. Parkes, who spoke Chinese, became his principal negotiator. The Arrow War dragged on for years, mainly because the British army was busy fighting the Indian Mutiny and the Manchus had the Taiping Rebellion on their hands.

Harry Parkes is looked upon by the Chinese as an arch-villain. In Chinese films he is portrayed leading cavalry charges and losing sword fights with mandarins. In reality he was an incompetent horseman and a non-combatant. During negotiations outside Peking, he was kidnapped, imprisoned and tortured, and most of his escort were murdered. This was against the international rules of war, which were, of course, unknown to the Chinese. Killing negotiators was a tactic of intimidation highly recommended in *The Art of War*.

To punish Emperor Hsien Feng (Xianfeng) for the murder of the Parkes party, which included Mr Bowlby, the war correspondent of *The Times*, Elgin burnt down the Summer Palace. He justified this act of vandalism to his general, Sir Hope Grant, by saying, "What would *The Times* say of me if I did not avenge its correspondent?"

The Earl of Elgin and Kincardine went into public service only because his father had spent a fortune shipping the Elgin Marbles from Greece to England. Before coming to China, Elgin was the Governor-General of Canada. He later became Viceroy of India.

*Above*: The Earl of Elgin signing the Treaty of Tientsin (Tianjin) in 1858. When Elgin's brother, Frederick Bruce, attempted to take the treaty to Peking for ratification, the Chinese fired on the British fleet from the Taku Forts and sank three British gunboats.

*Left*: Sir Harry Parkes (right) was involved in the *Arrow* incident. In the war he was seized by the Chinese during a truce. He was tortured and his colleagues murdered. This outrageous incident prompted Lord Elgin to burn down the Summer Palace as a reprisal.

*Opposite*: The ruined Bronze Temple at the Summer Palace. This photograph was taken a dozen years after it was burnt by Lord Elgin's forces. A Pekinese dog was "liberated" from the Summer Palace and given to Queen Victoria. She called the creature "Lootie."

*Above*: The allied headquarters at Canton. British and French forces occupied the city for three years after its capture. The Taiping Rebellion was raging throughout China, but foreign populations in the other four treaty ports were hardly affected by the fighting.

*Left*: Lord Elgin advancing on Peking. He refused to negotiate with the Chinese until Parkes and the other envoys were released. Of Parkes's party, only three British and seven Sikhs survived. The remaining seventeen—six British and eleven Sikhs—were murdered.

# Old Maps of China

Westerners tend to dismiss early Chinese maps as highly decorative scrolls with a mountain range at the top and the sea at the bottom. This southern ocean is often littered with small strange-shaped islands that are meant to represent Outer Barbarian countries like Britain, France, Holland and Sweden. In reality, the Chinese were quite capable of producing reasonably accurate maps as early as 300 BC, but like many other sciences mastered by the ancient Chinese, the skill of producing functional cartography seemed to have got lost somewhere over the years.

For centuries China appeared on Western maps as a vague landmass north of the Spice Islands, and until Matteo Ricci and the Jesuits started mapping the interior of China, the knowledge of European map makers was largely confined to the coastline. Even as late as 1816, when Captain Basil Hall sailed up the China coast in HMS *Lyra*, he found that these sea charts were often bewilderingly inaccurate. He wrote: "We discovered that according to one authority, we were sailing far up in the country, over wide forests and great cities; and according to another, the most honest author amongst them, our course lay directly through the body of a goodly elephant, placed in the centre of a district of country in token of the maker's candid confession of ignorance."

Even the great Matteo Ricci resorted to filling the empty wastes of Antarctica with fabulous beasts in his *Complete Map of the World*, which he made in 1602 for the Emperor Wan Li (Wanli). Western collectors are particularly fond of ancient maps that are decorated with splendid galleons, exotic mermaids, elegant compass roses, zephyrs and elaborate ornamental calligraphy. As a result, John Speed's *The Kingdome of China* is a connoisseur's delight. It has vignettes to cater to all tastes: curious native costumes, views of Macau and Quinzay (Hangzhou), Chinese wind-propelled carts and an execution. It even has a "parte of America" in the top right-hand corner.

*Right*: Théodore de Bry's *Amacao*, 1607, is the first Western engraving of Macau and is possibly the earliest printed China trade image. De Bry's engravings illustrated his books, *Grands Voyages* and *Petits Voyages*, which were published between 1590 and 1628.

*Opposite*: Jodocus Hondius's quarto map of China. Hondius's real name was Josse de Hondt. He engraved maps for other map makers like John Speed. He and his son Henricus became the leading map publishers in Amsterdam. In 1606, they published a new enlarged edition of Mercator's Atlas.

CHAP.6.§.3. *Errours of our Maps and Conceits of China.* 361

commonly call *Tartars*, with whom they haue alwayes had Warre, and once they wanne all the Kingdome from the *Chinois*.

For the Readers better satisfaction I haue here presented him *Hondius his Map of* China, *not to shew it, but the erroneous conceits, which all European Geographers haue had of it : A more complete Map of* China *I shall present after, as by comparison will appeare.*

### HONDIVS his Map of China.

This Kingdome standeth in an excellent climate and situation ; for besides the things which it hath in it selfe, it standeth very neere vnto *India*, and other Kingdomes, from whence commeth with great facilitie that which it desireth and wanteth. And before I passe any further, because I haue spoken of the situation and heigth of *China*, I will note for their sakes which would bee glad to learne, and also it may serue to mend two notable errours, which our newest Maps haue. The one is, That they make *China* a third part bigger then it is, placing this Citie of *Paquin* in fifty degrees, being in very deed but in forty onely, as we saw, which twice tooke the heigth thereof with a very good Astrolabe : And the limits and end of this Kingdome, which are three dayes iourney or lesse distant from this City of *Paquin*, are at the most but two degrees more : And so those great walls so famous in our *Europe* are in two and forty degrees; and this is the greatest heigth of the Kingdome of *China*.

The second errour is, that our Maps make a Kingdome aboue *China*, which they call *Catayo*, whereas indeed it is none other but this selfe same Kingdome of *China*: and the Citie of *Cambalu*, which they put for the head thereof, is this Citie of *Paquin* wherein wee are. Wee finde this here to be true very plainely by occasion of certaine newes which lately were spred ouer diuers parts by the way of *Mogor*, which gaue out many things, and great matters of *Catayo*, which seemed to be so peculiar and proper to this Kingdome of *China*, that they made vs doubt that

*Two notable errours of our newest Maps. Paquin in 40. degrees. The Kingdome of China goeth not past 42. degrees Northward. China and Catayo are all one. Cambalu and Paquin are all one.*

Abraham Ortelius's map of China was the first map of that country to appear in a European atlas. It was adapted from a map by Ludovico Giorgio, a Portuguese cartographer, who was a Spanish spy who purloined Portugal's maritime secrets.

*Left*: A detail of Ortelius's map of China, 1584. When information was lacking, cartographers added exotic animals and other decorations to fill the empty spaces. The "goodly elephants" featured here are probably the creatures mentioned by Captain Basil Hall.

*Below*: *The Kingdome of China* was produced by John Speed in 1626. It comes from his atlas, *A Prospect of the Most Famous Parts of the World*, which was the first world atlas to be published in England by an English cartographer.

*Opposite above*: Thomas Allom created this delightful print. His illustrations were based mainly on sketches by other artists, naval officers, soldiers and missionaries. Allom never visited China, but neither did Raphael or El Greco go anywhere near to Jerusalem.

*Opposite below*: A lantern painter's shop. The figure of the lantern painter was copied directly by Thomas Allom from a print by Pu Qua, published forty-three years earlier. Like Andy Warhol, Victorian printmakers frequently used "borrowed images."

*Right*: Victorian books on China were filled with small wood engravings similar to this one. A 600-page book might have as many as 150 of them. They were sometimes as small as a postage stamp and originally printed in black and white.

*Below*: During the Arrow War, British magazines sent war artists to China. Their sketches were reproduced by skilled wood engravers back in London. Photographs were also copied and engravings were made from them by hand until the necessary printing technology was successfully developed.

EAST IS EAST AND WEST IS WEST   91

# Chapter 2

# THE EMPIRE OF OPPORTUNITY AND THE TREATY PORTS
## (1860–1894)

The Chinese historian Li Chien-nung has classified this era (1860–1894) as "The Period of Imitation of Western Methods." The Treaty of Nanking (Nanjing) and the other treaties with the West were an attempt to "open up" China to the rest of the world. They attacked its traditional position of rigidly enforced isolationism. Chinese foreign policy had been summed up by Emperor Chien Lung (Qianlong) in his second edict to King George III in 1793: "Our Celestial Empire possesses all things in prolific abundance and lacks no product within its borders. There was therefore no need to import the manufactures of outside barbarians in exchange for our own produce."

After the Arrow War, China could not prevent change by burying its head in the sand like the proverbial ostrich. For good or evil, the country could no longer ignore global progress and change became unstoppable. Alien technology, ideas, politics and religion all left their mark. Initially, it was the missionaries who caused China the most problems. The Roman Catholic Church's crusade goes back to St Francis Xavier, whereas the Protestant invasion began with the arrival in China in 1807 of Robert Morrison of the London Missionary Society. The teachings of Christianity clashed with the annals of Confucius as interpreted by the Manchu and Chinese establishment. It was an assault on Confucian values with the missionaries preaching a form of sedition. The evidence to confirm this viewpoint was provided by the Hakka evangelist Hung Hsiu-chuan (Hong Xiuquan), who after studying Christianity under the American Baptist missionary, the Reverend Issachar Roberts, created his own cult of Christianity that resulted in the Taiping Rebellion which cost 20 million lives. Originally, the missionaries were confined to the treaty ports, but they tended to break the rules. For example, Abbé Chapdelaine lived illegally for three years in a small town in Kwangsi (Guangxi) province where he preached the Gospel. This was in direct violation of the Treaty of Whampoa (Whampo) of 1844 between France and China. His arrest and execution provoked the French into sending an army to support the British during the Arrow War.

The French were more interested in propagating the Catholic religion than in trade. The 1875 census reveals that out of 176 foreigners living in the French Concession in Shanghai, 132 were missionaries. The same census puts the foreign population of the International Settlement at a modest 2,297. This compares with about 100,000 in 1930. China's population in 1875 was about 400 million. The other treaty ports had far fewer foreign residents. A decade later, the number of Protestant missionaries re-corded in Szechwan (Sichuan), with a population of 20 million, was a mere 25. Contrary to popular histories, China was not swamped by missionaries and foreigners, but the problems they caused to the Manchu authorities were out of proportion to their numbers.

Christianity was not the only religion that created conflict in China in the nineteenth century: there were a number of serious Muslim rebellions and there were also the White Lotus Society and the triads. These were quasi-religious pro-Ming, anti-Manchu secret societies. The previous Ming dynasty had been founded by Hung Wu (Hongwu), a member of the Red Turbans, which was an offshoot of the White Lotus Society. In the Ching (Qing)

THE BATTLE OF MUDDY FLAT: April 4, 1854.

*Previous page*: Three high-ranking Chinese Ministers of State. Left to right: the President of the Board of War, the President of the Board of Finance and the President of the Board of Works. They were photographed by John Thomson in Peking (Beijing) in 1871.

*Left*: The Battle of Muddy Flat, 1854. This contemporary cartoon appeared in the *North-China Daily News & Herald*. Captains Kelly (center) and O'Callaghan (right) can be seen leading the attack on the imperial camp. On the city walls are the turbaned triads.

*Opposite above*: The Shanghai Municipal Police on parade in 1890. Captain J. P. McEuen, the Chief Superintendent of Police, can be seen on the right in uniform wearing a sword. It was a multi-national force composed mainly of British, Sikhs and Chinese.

dynasty, the White Lotus rebels almost captured Peking (Beijing) in 1813. In 1851, with the triads, they allied themselves to the Taipings. They were composed of a number of secret societies with varied religious practices.

It took longer for Western political thought to establish a bridgehead. The leader of the Reform Movement, Kang Yu-wei (Kang Youwei), a member of the literati, was impressed by the efficient way the Shanghai Municipal Council ran the International Settlement. It was about the only place in China where most of the roads were paved. His fellow reformer, Dr Sun Yat-sen, had been educated in Hong Kong and had lived in Hawaii and London. A third member, Charlie Soong, had attended a theological college in America. They sowed the seeds of the Chinese Revolution that overthrew the Ching dynasty. Sun and Soong were both Christians and triad members. It is not surprising that today's government in China treats any religion or cult with a suspicion that verges on paranoia.

The Shanghai Municipal Council, which Kang admired, came into being as the result of a skirmish in 1854 during the Taiping Rebellion. It was known as the Battle of Muddy Flat. The Small Swords, a band of Cantonese triads allied to the Taipings, had captured the walled city of Shanghai, located next to the foreign concessions. An imperial Manchu army arrived in force to retake the city.

The imperial soldiers seemed to have been more interested in looting the foreign concessions than fighting the triads. Things came to a head when a foreign resident was badly wounded protecting the virtue of a lady from a mob of Manchu bannermen. The British and American consuls asked the Manchu general to move his camp. He refused.

An Anglo-American force of 350 sailors and marines, together with the Shanghai Volunteers, attacked the camp containing 10,000 imperial troops. The Americans under Captain Kelly launched a frontal attack and the British under Captain O'Callaghan assaulted the Manchus' right flank. At the critical moment, the Small Swords appeared like the Seventh Cavalry on the left flank and the Manchus fled their camp. This is reputed to be the first time British and American forces had fought side by side in battle. The American Consul, R. C. Murphy, explained how it came about: "Kelly, O'Callaghan and I have been colloguing all afternoon, and the brogue rolled around us like a flood."

Shortly afterwards, a disturbed British admiral arrived on the scene. The British were officially neutral at this stage of the rebellion. Admiral Stirling felt obliged to support O'Callaghan's actions as the honor of a lady and the safety of British citizens had been involved, but the legality of the action was questionable.

N. O. Liddell, the Shanghai historian, explained: "He was firm in the conviction that the only legal call which would relieve him of the responsibility of taking part in a local conflict at Shanghai was the call of a Municipality. Thus it was that the Shanghai Municipality came into existence." Nobody quite understood the admiral's logic, but Edward Cunningham, the American Vice-Consul, supported the British admiral's idea: "Common law," he said enigmatically, "is better than a common head." The formation of the Shanghai Municipal Council gave (according to the admiral's theory) the foreign powers the right to defend, rule and administer the foreign concessions as an international municipality.

At the time, the Manchus were losing the civil war with the Taipings. By agreeing to the formation of the council, they hoped that the British, French and Americans would be forced to abandon their neutrality and support them. This plan eventually worked in spite of the Arrow War. In 1860, an American swashbuckler, Frederick Townsend Ward, raised a foreign mercenary force called the Ever-Victorious Army to defend Shanghai from the Taipings. A couple of years later, at the time of Ward's death, French and British forces were fighting on the side of the Manchus. Ward's mercenary army was later officered by British regulars under the command of the legendary Charles "Chinese" Gordon.

The Shanghai Municipal Council became an élitist quasi-democratic international body. A new council was elected by ratepayers every year. The chairman was generally a British or American Taipan. Out of it grew the International Settlement which became the model for the other larger treaty ports. Like any great city, it soon established its own police force, fire brigade, law courts, public works department and health department which was originally called Inspector of Nuisances. Education was left largely to the missionaries.

In the smaller treaty ports, the foreign consuls endeavored to control their nationals. The treaties had granted foreigners extraterritorial rights. They were needed to protect their nationals from the vagary and brutality of Chinese law. Proof of guilt was based on obtaining a confession from the accused. Torture was used as a matter of course even on prosecution witnesses. Barbarous punishments such as beheading, crucifixion and the death of a

*Above*: A Manchu bannerman armed with an old-fashioned matchlock musket. On his belt he carries his spare cartridges. This soldier was a member of the Peking garrison in the early 1870s. His barracks were situated in the Tartar City.

THE EMPIRE OF OPPORTUNITY AND THE TREATY PORTS   95

Many houses built in Southern China with European architectural features had traditional Chinese ground plans and contained numerous courtyards. These mansions were inhabited by generations of an extended family. Each family branch had its own quarters.

*Left*: An early panorama of the busy waterfront at Canton (Guangzhou) taken in the 1870s. Hundreds of river craft can be seen against a backdrop of Chinese and European buildings. The three tall buildings are fortified pawnshops.

*Opposite below*: A formal portrait of three Cantonese ladies resplendent in their gorgeous finery with a servant standing behind them. Their tiny bound feet peek out from beneath their skirts. The lady in the center has a long fingernail protected with a sheath.

thousand cuts were totally unacceptable to the West.

Foreign nationals were tried by their consuls. Justice varied. The consuls of some countries would award punishments that were little more than a slap on the wrist for their wayward nationals for crimes that would earn an offender five years in jail if they were of a different nationality. Some countries did not even have resident consuls. The system was constantly abused. For instance, there was the case of an Irish madam who married an Italian stoker in order to become an Italian citizen, thus avoiding being deported by the British. The Italian Consul's attitude toward houses of ill fame was more cavalier than that of his puritan English counterpart. Petty offenders like the lady in question could always seek refuge in the French Concession where 250 brothels operated openly. Mixed courts were established, under a Chinese judge and a foreign assessor, which generally dealt with commercial disputes between the two communities.

In the early years, the foreign population of the treaty ports was composed mainly of consular officials, customs officers, missionaries, doctors, merchants and sailors who had jumped ship. As commerce developed, bankers, architects, engineers, artisans, tradesmen, businessmen and entrepreneurs of all kinds arrived. With them came adventurers, carpetbaggers, remittance men and dubious fortune hunters. China was seen as an empire of opportunity. To the businessmen, it was a vast emporium of unlimited potential wealth. The missionaries took another viewpoint. Saving souls was their priority. To quote H. Grattan Guinness's hymn, "The Voice of Thy Brother's Blood": "A million a month in China are dying without God!"

An English tea merchant playing the scissors-stone-paper finger game at a Chinese banquet. His Chinese host is seen winning the round. This game is still popular in China today. On the right, a sing-song girl entertains the guests.

THE EMPIRE OF OPPORTUNITY AND THE TREATY PORTS

# The Beginning of the Missionary Invasion

Missionaries were regarded as troublemakers by the mandarins, the East India Companies and the opium taipans. When the London Missionary Society sent Robert Morrison to China, the John Company refused to let him travel on one of their ships. Morrison was a very determined man. In 1807, he arrived in China via New York aboard an American vessel.

Morrison was the first Protestant missionary in China. He compiled the first English–Chinese dictionary and was the first person to translate the Bible into Chinese. He became so proficient in the language that Sir George Staunton, also a brilliant linguist who, as a boy, had accompanied Macartney's mission to China, persuaded the John Company to employ him.

Sir George, as a John Company man, was not inclined to rock the boat. The mandarins used Chinese linguists, who spoke only pidgin. They were uneducated and unable to understand an official document, let alone translate it into English. This caused innumerable problems. They commonly used the pidgin phrase "can do," which meant "yes," but sometimes "no," in the way the Spanish word *mañana*, which literally means "tomorrow" but all too often means "this year, next year, sometime, never."

Morrison upset the mandarins by translating Lord Napier's blunt, angry words literally, without diplomatically softening them. He founded the Anglo-Chinese College in Malacca whose students included the American William Hunter, and Karl Gutzlaff, a Pomeranian saddle-maker turned missionary.

Gutzlaff spent much of his time aboard the *Sylph*, an opium smuggling ship owned by William Jardine, preaching Christianity to the Chinese while selling them opium. He also dabbled in espionage.

He printed thousands of religious tracts, which he gave to his converts to distribute. These venal rice-Christians, so-called because they changed their religion for a bowl of rice, sold them back to his printer, who resold them to Gutzlaff. This frustrated his grand design "to evangelize *en masse* a great nation."

Morrison, as a missionary, was also not a bewildering success. In twenty-seven years of pious endeavor, he managed to convert only four Chinese to Christianity.

A wood engraving of a Bible reading on a Chinese farm that appeared in Geraldine Guinness's *In the Far East*. This missionary's popular book sold over 100,000 copies. It was distributed by the East London Institute for Home and Foreign Missions.

*Right*: The Lord's Prayer in Chinese. The missionaries printed thousands of religious tracts.

*Far Right*: The Chinese Religious Tract Society's leaflet entitled "No. 6. True Happiness." Over half the population of Ching dynasty China were illiterate.

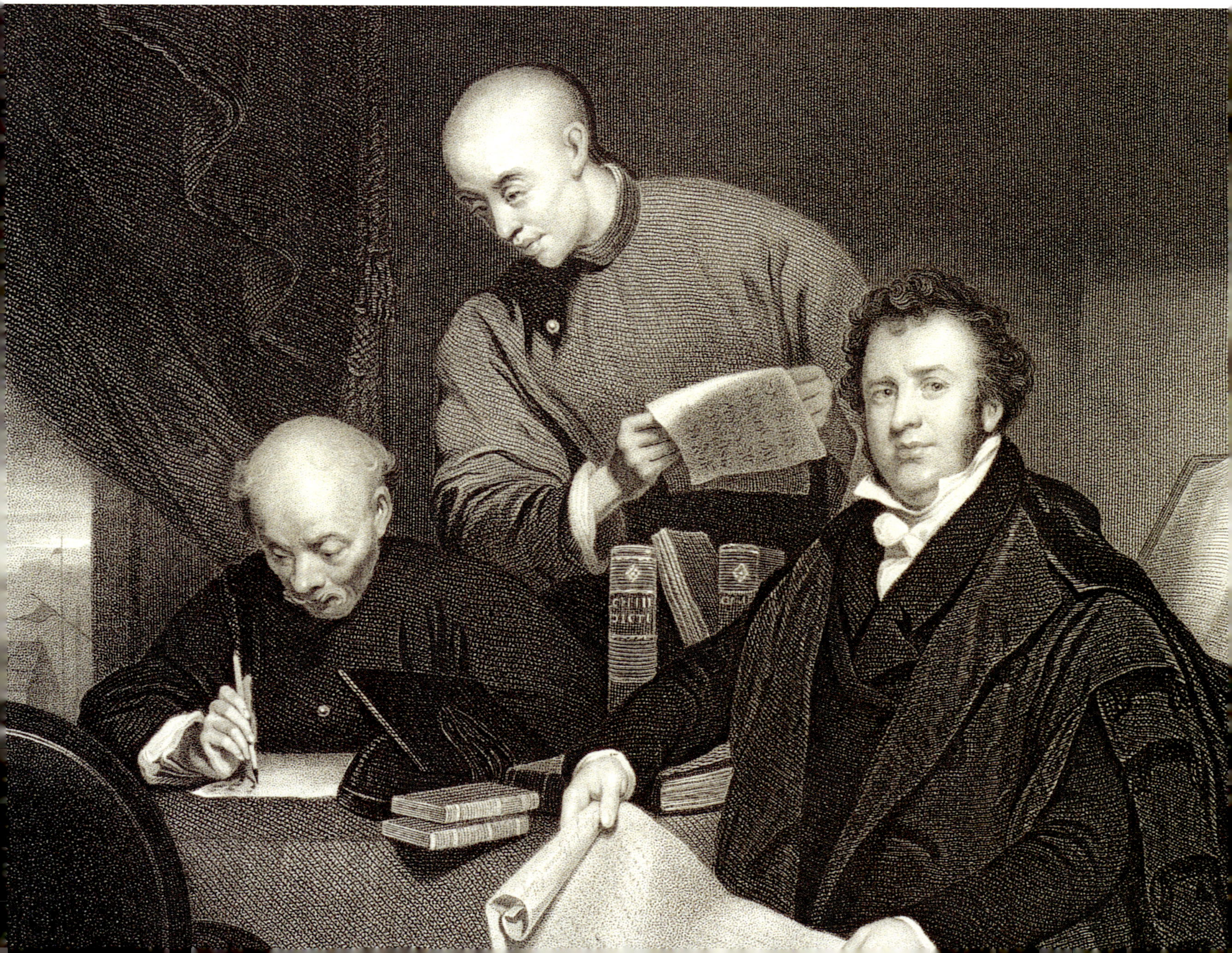

*Below*: Robert Morrison with his assistants who helped him to translate the Bible into Chinese. The engraving is from a painting by George Chinnery, the English artist, who is famous for his paintings of China and Macau around the time of the Opium War.

THE LORD'S PRAYER.

我父在天願爾名聖爾國臨格爾旨得成在地如在天焉我儕所需之糧今日賜我免我儕諸負如我免負我者尤毋導我於誘惑乃拯我出於惡蓋國也權也榮也皆歸於爾爰及世世誠心所願

中國聖教書會印發

福

求福○蓋聞多福之頌祝於康衢求福之詩興於葛藟世人每以多財多子輒稱之曰有福如於失意時忽得橫財則曰轉禍爲福如大難不死則曰必有後福此皆指世上之福而言非眞福也夫眞福不在此而在蒙主赦罪之恩在得重生在與主復和此非暫時之福乃永久之眞福也歷千萬年不壞特世人昧於所求每向木偶跪拜其中心以爲不如是不能邀福而孰知天父掌禍福之權故不求天父而求木偶者不但不能得福且延永刑焉然則何能免此曰有法及早悔改轉移而信耶穌則在世得安樂之福死後享永生之福以耶穌爲眞神之子爲救世之主故耳信之者無不可免罪得永生焉耶穌曰凡勞苦任重者歟就我我則我賜爾安蓋我心溫柔謙遜爾負我軛而學我則必獲安於爾靈蓋我軛易我負輕也故凡欲求福者宜反其向之所求轉意而誠求救主則永福無有不得者焉

NO. 6. TRUE HAPPINESS—PUBLISHED BY THE CHINESE RELIGIOUS TRACT SOCIETY.

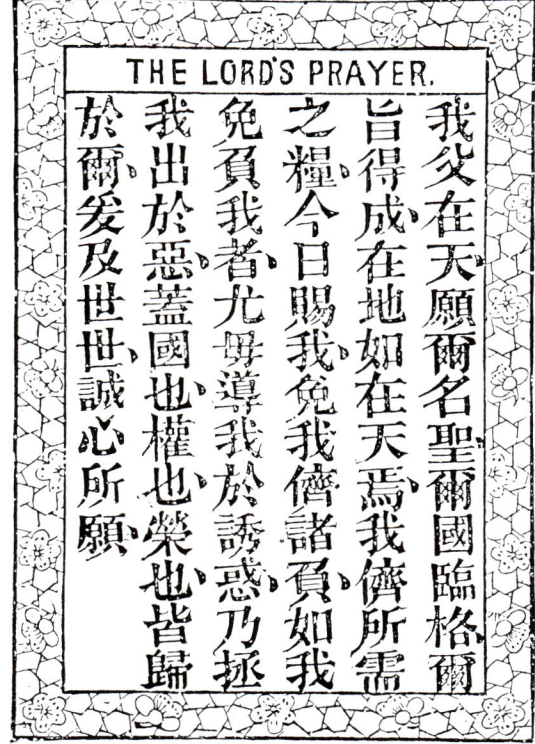

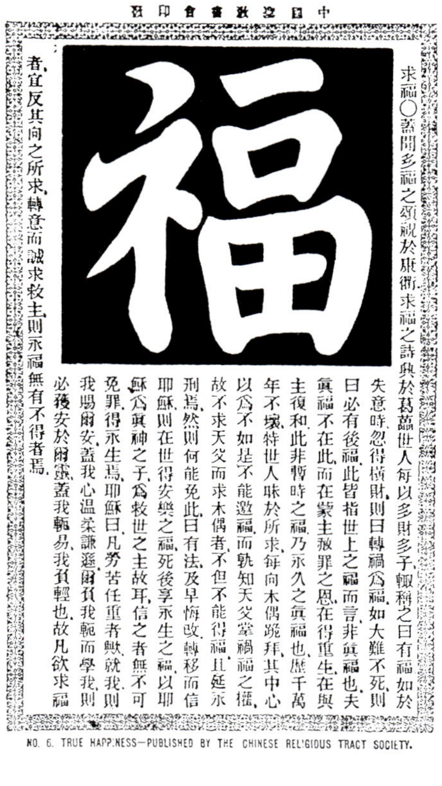

*Right*: Missionaries distributing rice to potential rice-Christians at a temple in Canton during the Arrow War. Missionaries have distributed Christian aid for generations. The missionaries of today concentrate more on feeding the hungry than on saving their souls.

*Below*: Shanghai Cathedral was designed by Sir George Gilbert Scott. He was also responsible for the Albert Memorial and St Pancras Station in London. Sir George is often confused with his grandson, Sir Giles Gilbert Scott, the architect of Liverpool Cathedral.

*Opposite above*: Karl Gutzlaff acting as an interpreter between Commodore Sir J. J. Gordon Bremer and Chinese mandarins at a conference in Chusan (Zhoushan). Because Gutzlaff spoke fluent Chinese, Captain Elliot appointed him Chief Magistrate of Chusan during the British occupation.

*Opposite below*: The London Missionary Society was founded in 1795. This copy of their publication *Missionary Sketches*, featuring a map of Canton, was published in 1835, the year after their most celebrated member, Dr Robert Morrison, died.

*Below*: Protestant missionaries in Chinese costume. It was quite common for missionaries to wear Chinese clothes, especially in the remoter regions where most of the inhabitants had never seen a European.

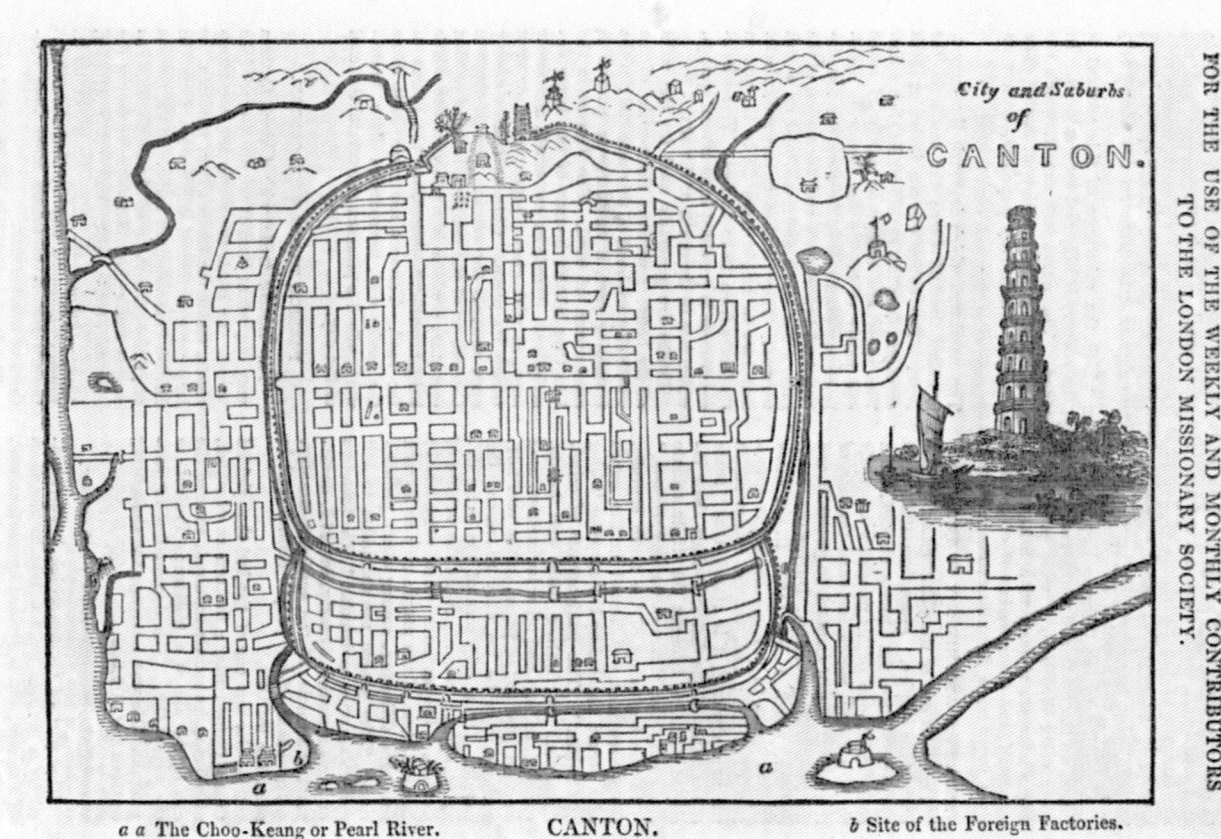

THE EMPIRE OF OPPORTUNITY AND THE TREATY PORTS    103

# The Taiping Rebellion (1851–1864)

Hung Hsiu-chuan (Hong Xiuquan), an embittered, failed civil service candidate, studied Christianity under the Reverend Issachar J. Roberts, an American Baptist Minister. Hung had a dream that convinced him that he was the brother of Jesus Christ. He founded a semi-Christian movement known as the Heavenly Kingdom of Great Peace, or Taiping. Attempts to suppress it by the Manchus led to a rebellion that cost 20 million lives and devastated China for thirteen years.

The Taipings were anti-Buddhist, anti-Taoist, anti-Confucian and anti-Manchu. They were also anti-Catholic and anti-French. This at first endeared them to American and British missionaries. They regarded the Taipings as Chinese Protestants, if somewhat unorthodox and socialist.

The Taipings were joined by the anti-Manchu secret societies whose war cry was "Rebel against the Ching, restore the Ming." Together they captured over 600 cities, including Nanking, which became their capital. The Manchu forces lost complete control and their credibility was destroyed, but they were rescued by the Chinese literati, who loathed the Taipings even more than the Manchus. They raised two formidable Chinese armies, the Hunan and Anhwei (Anhui), which closed on Nanking.

Internal strife had weakened the Taipings after Hung had murdered his best generals. His theocratic administrative system was a total failure and resented. He lost many of his foreign supporters after a visit by Roberts to Nanking. "I believe that he is crazy," Roberts wrote, describing the Heavenly King, "especially in religious matters." The fact that Hung had 600 women and 68 wives at his disposal may have offended the worthy American Baptist Minister.

When the forces of the only surviving competent Taiping general, Prince Li, threatened Shanghai, Chinese merchants raised foreign mercenary armies to defend it. They were commanded by American, British and French officers. Nanking was besieged by the Hunan, Anhwei and mercenary armies. The Heavenly King committed suicide, Nanking was captured and the rebellion collapsed.

Hung Hsiu-chuan, known as the Heavenly King, was the founder of the semi-Christian movement called the Taiping, or Heavenly Kingdom of Great Peace. Twenty million Chinese died in the Taiping Rebellion, which raged for thirteen years.

*Top*: The Heavenly King lived in splendor in this magnificent palace in Nanking with his 600 women and 68 wives. This drawing was made by Frederic Le Breton Bedwell during Admiral Sir James Hope's diplomatic mission in 1861.

*Left*: Le Breton Bedwell's drawing of the "Inspector of the Heavenly Custom House" at Nanking. He provided the British sailors with a pass. They visited the Reverend Issachar J. Roberts, the Heavenly King's foreign adviser, who "wore a yellow robe and tinsel crown."

*Above*: The Porcelain Tower at Nanking was a 250-foot hexagonal structure. In 1842, Sir Henry Pottinger stationed a guard to protect this pagoda from being looted by British soldiers and sailors. It was later destroyed by the Taipings.

*Left*: Taiping chieftains and rebel soldiers in Nanking. The Taipings wore their hair long as a gesture of defiance against the hated Ching emperors who compelled their Chinese subjects to wear a queue and shave their foreheads in the Manchu style.

106 CHINA ILLUSTRATED

CHINESE ARCHER.

MILITARY MANDARINS.

*Above and left*: The soldiers of the imperial Chinese army were known as bannermen. The principal force, the Eight Banners, was composed of Manchus, Mongolians and the descendants of the Chinese who had supported the Manchus when they overthrew the Ming dynasty.

# The Ever-Victorious Army

After the Taipings' allies, the Small Swords, had captured the walled city of Shanghai, the Manchu officials and merchants sought refuge in the nearby Foreign Settlements. The Manchus and French eventually recaptured the walled city, but many Chinese remained in the Settlements.

One of these, Yang Fang, a rich banker, raised a foreign mercenary force to protect the city when it was threatened by the loyal Prince Li. The force's commander was the American adventurer, Frederick Townsend Ward. Initially, he recruited his mercenaries from the scum of Shanghai's waterfront.

Ward easily captured a few small towns, but his night attack on Sung-chiang was a disaster. It was meant to be a surprise attack, but his army of noisy drunks alerted the Taipings and were slaughtered.

After this defeat, he built up a new force of foreign-trained Chinese soldiers. This became known as the Ever-Victorious Army. Ward was killed while capturing Tzu-chi and was succeeded by another American, Henry Burgevine, who was a disaster.

The Chinese did not like Burgevine, so they stopped the army's pay. Consequently, he stormed into the paymaster's office, beat him up and then deserted to the Taipings. He was replaced by a British Army officer, Major Charles Gordon.

Within ten days, "Chinese" Gordon had put together a flotilla of makeshift gunboats and captured Fushan. He was a stickler for discipline and refused to let his troops loot, plunder or rape. Ward's officers and many Chinese troops deserted. Gordon recruited British regulars to replace the officers and hired captured Taipings as foot soldiers. Li Hung-chang (Li Hongzhang), the commander of the Anhwei army, was horrified. Gordon's campaign was a success and he was made a general by the Chinese.

Meanwhile, Burgevine deserted from the Taipings. The rogue then suggested to Gordon that together they should use the Ever-Victorious Army to seize power in China. For fear of the army falling into unscrupulous hands, Gordon and Li Hung-chang disbanded it without consulting their superiors.

Gordon, a great Victorian hero, was killed years later defending Khartoum, and Li Hung-chang became the most powerful man in China.

*Far left*: Li Hung-chang was the commander of the Anhwei army. After the Manchu generals had failed to suppress the Taipings, Li and Tseng Kuo-fan (Zeng Guofan), both ethnic Chinese, defeated the rebels with the aid of the Ever-Victorious Army.

*Left*: General "Chinese" Gordon dressed in the Order of the Yellow Jacket. It was awarded to him for the part he played in defeating the Taipings. Gordon refused, on principle, to accept a further monetary reward of $10,000 for his services.

*Right*: Henry Andrea Burgevine succeeded Ward as commander of the Ever-Victorious Army. This explosive adventurer changed sides several times and was known in Shanghai as "The Double Chrysanthemum." He drowned in mysterious circumstances.

*Far right*: Frederick Townsend Ward, the swashbuckling American mercenary who founded the Ever-Victorious Army. His use of gunboats to attack walled cities was highly successful. After his death in battle, he was replaced by Burgevine, then Gordon, who refined Ward's tactics.

Burgevine

*Left*: These veterans of the Ever-Victorious Army were photographed by John Thomson a decade after the end of the Taiping Rebellion. The Taipings called them "Imitation Foreign Devils" because of their green European-style uniforms.

*Below*: General Gordon's artillerymen were supplied with guns and ammunition by the British. Their commander, Major Frederick Tapp, was a brilliant officer. His death "was a calamity equal almost to the loss of a battle," wrote Gordon's biographer, A. Egmont Hake.

# Sir Robert Hart of the Chinese Imperial Maritime Customs

During the occupation of the walled city of Shanghai by the Small Swords, the mandarins were unable to collect customs dues. In desperation, they asked the foreign consuls for help. In its first year, the foreign-run Imperial Maritime Customs at Shanghai collected a million taels of silver in revenue, far more than the corrupt mandarins had done previously.

The new customs service was not popular with the foreign traders who complained that the Inspector General, Horatio Nelson Lay, "was too strong to be bullied and too honest to be bribed" and "was incapable of telling the difference between a simple clerical error and fraud." After Lay had been attacked in the street and seriously wounded, he was replaced by a young Irishman called Robert Hart, a former British Consulate interpreter.

Hart spoke excellent Chinese, albeit with an Irish accent, and English with a singsong Chinese accent. His customs service eliminated much of the friction between foreigners and the mandarins, as well as generated more revenue, so it was extended to the other treaty ports.

"China's oldest friend" became an institution and advised both the British and the Ching government for fifty years. He loved female company: "He would almost purr over women." He even had his own band. He was popular with almost everybody except his own staff, who loathed him. They were underpaid and overworked. Every year they waited nervously for his birthday: it was the day he promoted people, generally his relatives. Like Queen Victoria, Hart had his own Birthday Honors List. He used to punish his subordinates by transferring them to some rat hole of a place, like Wuhu, where the Customs House was in danger of collapsing.

His reputation as a China expert suffered when he failed to predict the Boxer Rebellion. But the aged autocratic spin doctor managed to save face by announcing, "The more I know of China, the less I seem to know," not particularly original—even in 1900.

Sir Robert Hart replaced Horatio Nelson Lay, who had been knifed in the street, as Inspector General. Known as the "I.G." Hart served the Ching government faithfully for over fifty years. This caricature appeared in the English weekly magazine, *Vanity Fair*, in 1894.

110 CHINA ILLUSTRATED

*Left*: Sir Robert Hart's Chinese band was known as the "I.G.'s Own." They gave an open-air concert in the inspectorate garden every Wednesday afternoon. The Portuguese bandmaster, M. Encarnacao, stands on the left of the band and Sir Robert on the right.

*Center left*: The gateway of Hart's house in Peking after it had been rebuilt. It had been burnt down during the Boxer Rebellion. The plan of the building was in the shape of an "H" (for Hart) and was reconstructed on the original foundations.

*Center right*: The second Customs House was built in 1894 on the site of the old Chinese building on the Bund. The clock tower was 110 feet high. This unsightly Victorian gothic red brick monstrosity was replaced by a new building in 1927.

*Below*: The original Chinese Customs House in Shanghai was the headquarters of the first foreign Inspector General of the Imperial Chinese Customs, Horatio Nelson Lay. He was totally incorruptible and the scourge of the crooked taipans and mandarins alike.

THE EMPIRE OF OPPORTUNITY AND THE TREATY PORTS

# Ching Peking

Victorian travelers tended to be rather disappointed with Peking. They were impressed by its massive walls, but the inner city was not as they had imagined it. The photographer John Thomson wrote: "There is hardly a spot in the capital that does not make one long for a single glimpse of that Chinese paradise we had pictured to ourselves in our youth—for the bright sky, the tea-fields, orange-groves and hedges of jasmine, and for the lotus-lakes filling the air with their perfume."

Visitors were appalled by the weather, the dust storms and the streets that turned into quagmires when it rained, the smell of camel dung, and worse, the terrifying cold of winter and the unbearable heat in summer.

The great city of Kublai Khan was becoming rather shabby. The magnificent buildings were still there, but the majority of the houses were only one story high. Ching Peking was divided into two. There was the Chinese City where the ethnic Chinese lived, and the Tartar City of the Manchu bannermen, the prince's palaces, temples, libraries, government buildings and the foreign legations.

Ching Peking was a city of well-organized ghettos each protected by a dividing wall.

Inside the Tartar City was the Imperial City, with its great lakes. It was here that Marco Polo met Kublai Khan in his lakeside palace. Centuries later, Emperor Kuang Hsu (Guangxu) was imprisoned here by the Empress Dowager Tzu Hsi (Cixi), who did not approve of his reforms. In the middle of the Imperial City was the Great Within or Forbidden City, where the emperors lived in an earthly paradise surrounded by their wives, concubines and eunuchs.

The temples and the magnificent palaces were dutifully admired, but it was the inhabitants, the curio shops and the camels that seemed to have attracted the attention of foreign tourists the most. The great American travel writer, Eliza R. Scidmore, wrote: "Nowhere in China is street life so busy, bright and picturesque as Peking, with such unceasing variety of type and costume, incident and display." This was written before the Forbidden City, in all its glory, was open to the public.

**This ground plan of the Imperial Palace in Peking was drawn by John Nievhoff, the steward of the Dutch embassy of 1655. He wrote that it "far exceeds all Royal Palaces in Europe for Splendour, Art, Wealth and Pleasure."**

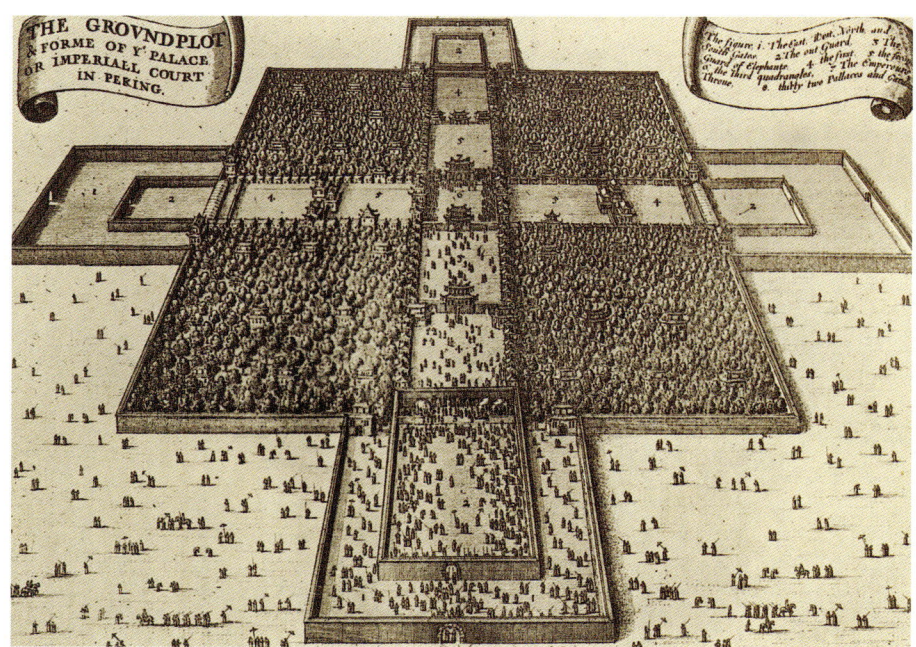

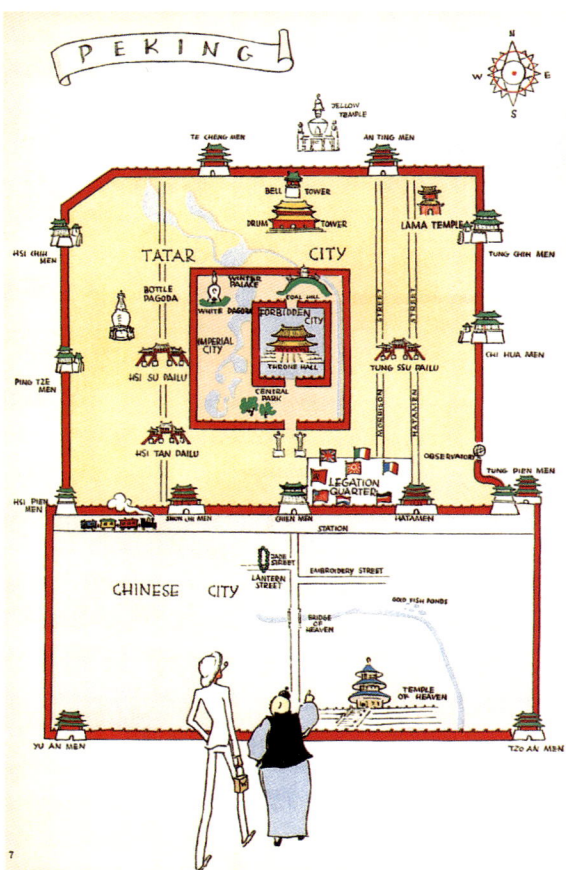

*Top*: The massive 40-foot walls of the Chinese City were impressive, but failed to keep out attacking armies. Chairman Mao ordered them demolished because they symbolized the feudal past of imperial China.

*Left*: A charming map of Peking by the Austrian cartoonist Friedrich Schiff, showing the location of the four walled cities: the Forbidden City, the Imperial City, the Tartar City and the Chinese City.

*Above*: This hand-colored postcard shows the entrance to the Forbidden City during the Ching dynasty when the Empress Dowager, Tzu Hsi, held sway over China in the early days of the twentieth century. The Forbidden City is also known to the Chinese as the Great Within.

THE EMPIRE OF OPPORTUNITY AND THE TREATY 113

A courtyard in the Forbidden City. It was a part of the emperor's palace where he lived surrounded by his empresses, concubines and eunuchs. Nobody except the emperor's close relatives or high ministers of state were allowed to enter.

*Above left*: The Mongol dynasty Bell Tower contains the heaviest bell in China. There were problems with casting it. After a number of failures, success was achieved only after the daughter of the master bell-maker hurled herself into the molten bronze during casting.

*Above*: Traveling antiques dealers displaying their wares. The Chinese City in Peking was the center of China's curio and antiques trade. Different streets were devoted to particular collectables, such as jade, porcelain and embroidery.

*Left*: "The marble bridge in the picture contains seventeen arches and is the finest that I have seen in China or indeed in the East," wrote the photographer John Thomson in the 1870s, when herds of deer still roamed the ruins of the Summer Palace.

THE EMPIRE OF OPPORTUNITY AND THE TREATY PORTS

The Temple of Heaven was the most sacred building in imperialist China. It was necessary for every emperor, be he Han Chinese, Mongol or Manchu, to worship there at least twice a year in order to maintain the Mandate of Heaven.

# The First Treaty Ports

With the exception of Shanghai, the original five treaty ports were not very successful at first. The mob had burnt down the Canton (Guangzhou) factories during the Arrow War, so Harry Parkes suggested to the Manchu authorities that Shamien (Shameen), an almost uninhabited sandbank pretending to be an island, would be a less vulnerable location for a foreign concession. The reclamation was finished in 1861, but there was a general exodus after a riot in 1883 when thirteen buildings were burnt down by the Cantonese mob. Hong Kong and Shanghai were safer places to trade.

Initially, the only other British consuls were at Foochow (Fuzhou), Amoy (Xiamen) and Ningpo (Ningbo). They were H. Grimble, a former ship's captain who could not speak Chinese. Unfortunately, his linguists spoke only pidgin and Cantonese, which was not very useful in Foochow. He was soon replaced. G. T. Lay, a former Bible salesman, was sent to Amoy, and Robert Thom, who had translated *Aesop's Fables* into Chinese, to Ningpo. Both were good linguists but both died shortly after being appointed.

Britain had been granted extraterritorial rights. This meant that British nationals could be tried only by their fellow countrymen. The mandarins expected the consuls not only to control the behavior of drunken British sailors, crooked merchants and fanatical missionaries, but also held them responsible for the behavior of all foreigners over whom, of course, they had no legal authority at all.

After a chaotic start, the treaty ports prospered and increased in number, and by the end of the century there were thirty-seven foreign concessions all over China, from Chungking (Chongqing) on the far side of the Three Gorges, to the Yellow Sea. There were large prosperous ports like Tientsin (Tianjin), which had been laid out by "Chinese" Gordon, and perpetual trouble spots like Ichang (Yichang), which did not even possess a hotel. Germany acquired Tsingtao (Qingdao) as a naval base, which became famous for its eccentric German architecture and splendid beer.

*Opposite above*: The formidable German gun emplacements on Bismarck Hill overlooking Tsingtao were not formidable enough to prevent Japanese and British forces capturing them in a night attack at the beginning of World War I, in November 1914.

*Above*: The Germans turned Tsingtao into a fortified garden city. Even today it is dominated by its Teutonic architecture. In spite of three decades of Japanese occupation and over half a century of Chinese rule, much is still visually a German city.

*Left*: The city of Amoy can be seen in the distance behind a massive boulder which the Europeans called "Six-mile Rock." Amoy is littered with these enormous boulders, many of which are connected by legend to the famous pirate Koxinga (Guoxingye) and local hero.

THE EMPIRE OF OPPORTUNITY AND THE TREATY PORTS

Manchu artillerymen on guard in the garden of the British consulate at Canton. When this picture was taken in the 1870s, the Tartar garrison numbered 1,800. Canton had a population of around a million residents at the time.

*Right*: A chromolithograph of Canton from a painting by Chun Ling Soo, ca. 1845, showing the busy river traffic and the waterfront. The foreign factories (right), burnt down during the Arrow War, are flying their flags.

*Below left*: A view of Shamien in the late 1860s. The small Anglican Church can be seen behind the sampans. The concession was famous for its charming English rose garden and graceful French and English colonial Victorian architecture.

*Below right*: The dynamic and controversial Sir Harry Parkes, the founder of Shamien. He later became the British Minister in Japan during the Meiji Restoration. His final appointment was as British Minister in China, where he died in office in 1885.

THE EMPIRE OF OPPORTUNITY AND THE TREATY PORTS

*Left*: Nanking Road was a modest little street around 1900. It developed later into the Bond Street and Fifth Avenue of Shanghai rolled into one, with its fabulous Chinese department stores: Wing On, Sincere and Sun Sun.

*Below*: Will's Bridge in Shanghai has been described as "the more or less illegitimate ancestor of the present Garden Bridge." This privately owned toll bridge spanned the Soochow Creek. The first replacement bridge collapsed during construction.

*Above*: The ancient walled city of Shanghai. The walls were constructed in the fourteenth century and were not demolished until after China became a republic. The city was a part of the Chinese Municipality and was separate from the International Settlement.

*Left*: The southern end of the Shanghai Bund of the International Settlement in 1872. The elegant colonial architecture is typical of the period when the buildings were seldom taller than three stories. The Bund was a towing path before Shanghai became a treaty port.

THE EMPIRE OF OPPORTUNITY AND THE TREATY PORTS

A picturesque junk on the Min River above Foochow, which was the major tea port of southern China during the nineteenth century. The Min River is navigable 300 miles inland. It was famous for its photogenic scenery.

Nanking Arsenal was built by Li Hung-chang in his campaign to modernize the weaponry of the Ching army. It stood near to the ruins of the Porcelain Tower, which had been destroyed during the Taiping Rebellion.

*Left*: The prosperous Foreign Settlement at Foochow. In the middle of the nineteenth century, this treaty port became the center of the tea trade. It was the capital of Fukien province where the popular Bohea tea was grown.

*Below*: The clippers *Ariel* and *Taeping* battle it out in the English Channel. The first three clippers docked on the same tide. It had taken them 99 days to sail 15,000 miles from Foochow to London. Controversially, the *Taeping* was declared the winner.

THE EMPIRE OF OPPORTUNITY AND THE TREATY PORTS

*Opposite*: This sketch of a corner of a Chinese tea garden was made by the artist C. D. Weldon, who illustrated Julian Ralph's book, *Alone in China*. In the 1890s, he accompanied the author on a trip in the houseboat *Swallow* down the Grand Canal.

*Above*: The Willow Tea House in Shanghai. Legend has it that this famous building was used as the model for the famous Willow Pattern design. This blue-and-white porcelain was imported into England where the design was copied by Thomas Minton in 1780.

*Right*: A tea-tasting room in Canton in the 1870s. The screened windows faced north to give an even light when the tea was being examined. Standard tea-tasting cups were used. The canisters on the shelves contained registered samples of teas from previous years.

THE EMPIRE OF OPPORTUNITY AND THE TREATY PORTS 131

# Transport in the Middle Kingdom

There is a popular misconception that the rickshaw is of Chinese origin. In fact, it was invented by Jonathan Goble, an American Baptist missionary in Japan, whose wife considered it degrading for a Christian to be carried in a sedan chair by two sweating coolies. In Japanese, the word *jinrikisha* means man-power-vehicle, or as Victorian wits were wont to say, a "Pullman car." This early example of Yankee cultural imperialism arrived in Shanghai in 1874.

Sedan chairs had been around for ever. They ranged from the elaborate palanquins of the mandarins and emperors to the humble hire-chair. There was also the wheelbarrow, invented by Ko Yu in the first century BC. This common mode of transport had an enormous wheel in the middle and was used not only as a goods vehicle but as a six-seater bus. The more sophisticated models came with a sail and mast. Horse transport was less popular because the Peking cart had no springs and was horrendously uncomfortable.

China had a very extensive network of waterways. Whenever possible, the Chinese built their cities on a river or canal. Most goods were transported by water and millions of people lived aboard junks and sampans. There were houseboats, and even houses of ill-repute on boats, called flower boats. Junks came in all shapes and sizes and their design varied from province to province.

The Chinese had a hatred for railways. Jardines got permission to build a road from Shanghai to Woosung (Wusong) in 1876. They tried to deceive the authorities by building a railway instead, which, with diabolical cunning, they called a tramway. Photographs of the first engine, the Celestial Empire, show a tiny toy-town puff-puff. It had a maximum speed of 15 miles per hour. Jardines did not get away with their devious plan. The Chinese government was not fooled and promptly nationalized the line, ripped up the track and shipped everything lock, stock and barrel to Taiwan, where it was left to rust.

*Above*: The Peking cart had no springs. "Nothing can exaggerate the horrors of an unameliorated Chinese cart on an infamous road," wrote the celebrated traveler Isabella Bird, after breaking her arm in a Peking cart crash in Mongolia.

*Right*: The sampan was, and still is, the China boat-people's all-purpose small working vessel. It was the most common form of river transport. Sampans are propelled by a single oar in the stern. They were floating homes for millions of boat-people throughout China.

*Above*: A houseboat photographed around 1890. Expatriates living in the treaty ports frequently spent their holidays aboard such houseboats exploring China's rivers and canals. These vessels were generally towed by "trackers." Paddle steamers were rather rare.

*Left*: A wheelbarrow made for two. The Shanghai Municipal Council called them an "intolerable nuisance." To get rid of them, the council raised the license fee in 1895. There was a riot. The wheelbarrows survived and the whole council was forced to resign.

THE EMPIRE OF OPPORTUNITY AND THE TREATY PORTS

*Above*: The rickshaw arrived in Shanghai in 1874. It was invented by an American Baptist missionary, Jonathan Goble, in Japan. It became the principal mode of transport throughout China. Its successor, the pedicab, is still operating in many Asian countries.

*Right*: The first locomotive sent to China was the *Celestial Empire*. It had tiny 18-inch wheels and a top speed of 15 miles per hour. The engine made its first run in July 1876 taking 160 guests to Kiangwan. The journey of four and a half miles took 17 minutes.

*Top*: Chinese junks come in many forms. The shape of their bamboo sails varies enormously from province to province. Canal and river junks are flat-bottomed, unlike this typical bat-winged seagoing fishing junk from the Pearl River Delta.

*Left*: A young camel driver in front of the Great Wall of China. Camels were used to carry the riches of China along the Silk Road to the West. They were a common means of transport in northern China and Mongolia in the Ching dynasty.

*Above*: Sedan chairs date back to the days of the legendary Yellow Emperor. The emperors traveled in gorgeous palanquins carried by dozens of liveried bearers. The common sedan hire-chair was the taxi of China before the arrival of the rickshaw from Japan.

THE EMPIRE OF OPPORTUNITY AND THE TREATY PORTS 135

Peking Railway Station in the 1920s. It was estimated in 1900 that there was a mile of railway in China for every million inhabitants, whereas in Europe there were 2,400 people per mile of line. In imperial China, railways were identified with foreign domination by the ignorant masses.

*Above*: China ponies were used by Manchu military mandarins when on official business. This was considered appropriate because it was the Tartar cavalry who conquered China and overthrew the Ming emperors when establishing the Ching dynasty in 1644.

*Below*: A group of Belgian Shanghailanders pose for their picture in the public garden in the last days of the Ching dynasty. As more people owned cameras, amateur photographers were prepared to squander a bit of film on a fun family picture.

THE EMPIRE OF OPPORTUNITY AND THE TREATY PORTS 137

# Footbinding: Ching Dynasty Fashion Victims

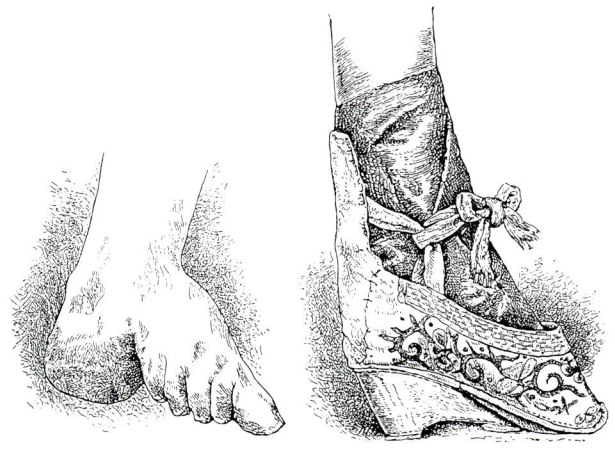

For a thousand years, basic Chinese female costume hardly changed. However, Manchu women were a different breed. They were hardy horsewomen rather than pampered hothouse plants. They did not bind their feet and had their own distinctive headdress. The basis was a strip of wood, ivory or precious metal around which the hair was twisted and then attached to the back of the head. It looked a little like a Stealth fighter decorated with flowers. Their allies, the Mongols, tended to wear fur hats. They were pragmatic people whose main concession to Chinese fashion was the use of expensive fabrics and exotic colors.

The wives and concubines of the rich Han Chinese were seldom seen in public but their coiffures were elaborate. They were confined to the women's quarter of a large family compound. Often the only males they saw were their husbands and their relatives. They dressed to please their man or mother-in-law rather than to attract the envy and admiration of other women.

Small feet were the criterion of true beauty. Footbinding was not the sole prerogative of the rich, although it indicated economic status. The process began at the age of four. The child went through two years of absolute agony until her feet became almost dead. They remained tightly bandaged until death. The tiny deformed feet were called "Golden Lilies." Sigmund Freud described footbinding as a "perversion that corresponds to foot-fetishism, it is only dirty and evil smelling feet that become sexual objects." He seems to have ignored the evidence of the "pillow books" that show that Chinese women did not take off their slippers when they had sex. Their feet were probably cleaner than those of the *hausfraus* of Vienna.

The young lady shown below who allowed her naked foot to be photographed by John Thomson was an exception. Thomson noted that her tiny odoriferous foot when exposed neither looked like nor even smelled remotely like a fragrant lily.

*Above:* This illustration, entitled "Golden Lilies—Bare and Shod," appeared in a children's book published by the London Missionary Society. It devotes three pages to describing in terrifying detail the grim process of footbinding and the "indescribable torture" it caused the child.

*Left:* "Footbinding" by John Thomson, ca. 1871. Thomson had to pay an enormous bribe to photograph the deformed, naked foot of this forlorn fashion victim. There is an old Chinese saying that "For every pair of small feet there is a jar of tears."

*Opposite:* The most common form of female dress was the *samfoo*. It was a loose-fitting and somewhat shapeless outfit. This young girl's feet are not bound. Both sexes wore shoes or boots with white soles, sometimes as much as 3 inches thick.

*Opposite*: The daughters of a high Manchu court official showing their unique head-dress. The *cheongsam* is said to be derived from the long Manchu gown worn by these ladies. Unlike the Chinese, Tartar women did not bind their feet.

*Far left*: A young scholar. He is soberly dressed and carries a simple screen fan. The legendary Yellow Emperor is credited with inventing this kind of fan. The Japanese folding fan first appeared in China during the Ming dynasty.

*Left*: A Chinese merchant wearing a richly embroidered jacket, photographed by A. Hing. The display of conspicuous wealth is an indication of the sitter's character. A Chinese client generally wanted a full-face portrait that showed both ears.

*Below*: This collection of small photographs of Chinese beauties are called *cartes-de-visite*, which literally means "visiting cards," although they were seldom used as such. The photographs were mounted on card and given away to friends and family.

THE EMPIRE OF OPPORTUNITY AND THE TREATY PORTS 141

# Through China with a Camera (1868–1872)

In these days of the digital camera, it is difficult to appreciate the massive problems faced by the Victorian traveling photographer. When John Thomson and his two assistants, Akum and Ahong, went on a photographic expedition through China, they needed eighteen coolies to carry their equipment. In four years they covered 5,000 miles, from the rapids of the Yangtze River to the Great Wall.

Thomson used the wet collodion process. The glass negatives had to be sensitized and developed on the spot using a tent as a darkroom. Added to all of Thomson's problems was the reluctance of the Chinese to be photographed. Apart from the superstition that lenses were made out of babies' eyes, Thomson wrote that the Chinese regarded photography as "some black art, which at the same time bereft the individual depicted as so much of the principle of life as to render his death a certainty within a few short period of years."

He records that once while taking a picture of an old bridge at Chaochow, "a howling multitude came rushing down to where I stood near by the boat on the shore. Amid a shower of missiles I unscrewed my camera, with the still undeveloped photograph inside, took the apparatus under my arm and presented my iron-pointed tripod to the rapidly approaching foe, backed into the river and scrambled aboard my boat."

Thomson had the skill of putting his subjects at their ease so that they looked natural. This can be seen in conversation pieces like "Mr Yang's House." He also had the ability to strike up a rapport with his models, be they princes or beggars. He charmed Mr Yang, an enthusiastic amateur photographer himself, who let Thomson use his laboratory in his ladies' quarters. Yang was a collector of modern machinery, generally with disastrous results. The steam mining pump he installed somehow went into reverse and flooded the house. When Thomson left Peking in 1872, Yang was happily installing a "small gaswork."

**The bridge at Chaochow where John Thomson was attacked by a mob when taking this picture. The fragile glass negative somehow survived. The two ladder-like screens hanging in the arch were lowered at night as a flimsy protection against malignant spirits.**

*Left*: Mandarin Yang and his family, ca. 1871. An enthusiastic amateur photographer, Yang invited Thomson to use his laboratory, which was located in the ladies' quarters of his mansion in Peking. Thomson taught Yang how to prepare the chemicals used in photography.

*Below*: Street tradesmen in Kiukiang (Jiujiang). *Left to right*: Ahong with his mobile soup kitchen; a letter writer taking dictation from an illiterate lady; an itinerant barber; a wood-turner and his customer who is inspecting his work.

A Canton cargo junk. The design and rig of these picturesque craft varied enormously. A seagoing junk was very different from a flat-bottomed canal vessel. They were clumsy and slow-moving when compared with European ships.

*Opposite*: Jui-Lin, a Manchu and viceroy of the provinces of Kwangtung (Guangdong) and Kwangsi (Guangxi). He was aged 65 when this photograph was taken in 1870. With a fleet of modern gunboats, Jui-Lin almost succeeded in eliminating piracy in the region.

*Above*: Chinese actors playing a bride and groom in Ming dynasty marriage costume. As in this case, female characters were almost always played by young men or boys. There was no scenery used in Chinese drama, but the costumes were fabulous.

THE EMPIRE OF OPPORTUNITY AND THE TREATY PORTS

*Opposite*: Thomson sailed up the Yangtze River in Captain Yang's river junk in 1871 to photograph the Three Gorges. Mr Chang, Thomson's interpreter, is on the right. Captain Yang was seldom sober and Chang could not speak the local dialect.

*Above*: A Chinese artist in his studio. Thomson explained that these painters charged tourists by the foot for their canvases and worked "with wonderful speed." He did not think much of their portraiture, but he admired their paintings of ships.

# A Country of Clubs

It is said that when three Englishmen meet, they form a club. The object of the Victorian gentleman's club was to provide a congenial atmosphere for like-minded men to congregate and chat about subjects of mutual interest over a glass of good wine and tolerable food, free from the company of their wives and families.

The Shanghai Club on the Bund was modeled on this sort of establishment. It was notoriously difficult to join. It boasted of having the longest bar in the world and there seems to have been enough taipans to prop it up. Other foreigners warmed to this British obsession and formed their own national clubs and sports clubs.

Exercise was considered essential in order to survive the hostile climate. Almost every foreigner owned a China pony. These "furry little creatures" came from the wilds of Mongolia and were descended from Genghis Khan's cavalry ponies. At the first meeting of the Shanghai Race Club in 1848, Roman Nose beat Kiss-me-quick by a head in the Hack Stakes. The owners frequently rode their own ponies. In a few years, almost every major treaty port had a magnificent racecourse.

For fitness fanatics, there were places like the Ward Road Athletic and Social Club, where if you failed to keep in shape, the committee would arrive in your bedroom in the middle of the night and force you to box three rounds. One night they went to the wrong address and were attacked by an infuriated Irishman wielding a footbath.

The larger treaty ports had splendid recreation clubs, but in remote locations lateral thinking was required. In Ichang, there was no golf course, so in the dry season golfers used the dried-up bed of the Yangtze River, 40 feet below the level of the Bund, instead. Paul King, a golf enthusiast, explained, "It was the old original Scottish game, straight ahead for seven miles, with the bones of sunken junks and high stone boulders as 'hazards'—a unique and most exhilarating experience."

The grandstand at Hankow (Hankou). Almost every treaty port had a racecourse or held race meetings at one time or another. Bengal, known as "the Wonder Pony," who won 41 out of 42 starts, an all-China record, raced only in northern China.

*Top*: The annual dinner of the Shanghai Volunteers, held in the Shanghai Club in 1913. Unlike the Volunteers, in which anyone could serve, membership of the club was confined mainly to wealthy taipans and it was notoriously difficult to join.

*Above*: A group picture of the participants of the spring match between the Peking Golf and Country Club and the Parmachang Golf Club. It is interesting to note that there are two Japanese players in the photograph, which was taken in 1924.

*Left*: The Shanghai Club boasted of having the longest bar in the world. This essentially British establishment was on the Bund. Other countries followed the fashion with their own national clubs. There were numerous sporting clubs in every treaty port.

THE EMPIRE OF OPPORTUNITY AND THE TREATY PORTS   151

# Chapter 3

# THE END OF EMPIRE AND THE NEW REPUBLIC
(1894–1918)

"The Empire was not overthrown. It crumbled away," wrote Daniele Varè, an Italian diplomat. As a military race, the Manchus lost their credibility during the Taiping Rebellion, which had been put down by Chinese armies led by Chinese loyalist generals like Tseng Kuo-fan (Zeng Guofan) and Li Hung-chang (Li Hongzhang), aided by foreign forces. There were 10 million Manchus ruling 400 million Chinese and the Dragon Throne was unsteady. Britain and France would occasionally rock it a little when they wanted a concession, but the fall of the Dragon Throne was not in their interests. Neither Britain nor France had the military strength to occupy the Middle Kingdom on a permanent basis, even if they had wanted to.

Mother Russia, with her vast population, was a genuine threat. The imperial Russian empire had been expanding eastward into Asia for 400 years. In a clandestine conflict known as the "Great Game," Russia had been prevented by the British from invading India. Unable to penetrate the Himalayan mountain range, China became the softer option. During the negotiations at the end of the Arrow War (1856–60), Russia persuaded the Ching (Qing) government to cede to Russia the territory north of the Amur River, together with the Ussuri River provinces bordering on Korea. In 1860, Ensign N. V. Komarov and twenty-eight Russian soldiers landed on the Muravyov-Amursky Peninsula and established a modest military outpost, which in the next twenty years developed into the formidable naval base of Vladivostok.

For centuries China had treated the countries on her borders as vassal states. Some of them paid tribute to the Dragon Throne, but others did not. There were countries like Burma that fought three wars with British India before being finally being conquered in 1886. France grabbed Indochina and the Japanese had their eyes on the kingdom of Korea. Li Hung-chang, the leading statesman of the Empress Dowager Tzu Hsi (Cixi), was aware of China's military weakness compared to the might of the Western powers. He favored appeasement until China became strong, and attempted to build up a powerful navy, which was critical to China's defense. However, the emperor of Japan took his responsibilities more seriously than the empress dowager and Japan had become a formidable military power with foreign-trained forces when war broke out between the two countries in 1894 over Korea.

In spite of the plundering of naval funds by the empress dowager, China in theory had a more powerful fleet than Japan, but in practice because of official corruption it had very limited firepower. "The Chinese might have been victors at Yalu had their shells not been filled with sand—and even these ran out," wrote the British war correspondent Alfred Cunningham, who later founded the *South China Morning Post*. After losing the Battle of the Yalu River, the remains of the Chinese fleet withdrew to Weihaiwei (Weihai), where their commander, Admiral Ting, put up a tremendous fight defending the port, but the expected Chinese relief force never arrived.

Cunningham wrote, "Li Hung-chang, who had promised to send thousands of soldiers, did not send one man." Fighting against hopeless odds, Admiral Ting was eventually forced to surrender to the Japanese and then committed suicide.

Cunningham's admiration for the Chinese imperial

*Previous page*: The regent, Prince Chun, ruled imperial China from the death of the Empress Dowager Tzu Hsi until the overthrow of the Ching dynasty. He is seen here with his two sons. The child emperor, Pu Yi, is on the right.

*Above*: A skirmish between the Cossacks and the Japanese cavalry at the Battle of Telissu during the Russo-Japanese War.

*Right*: The defeated Russian commander General Stoessel drinks a toast with the victorious Japanese General Nogi during the surrender ceremony of the Russian garrison at Port Arthur in 1905. Both of Nogi's sons were killed during the siege.

*Far right*: Japanese infantry advancing during the Sino-Japanese War. After the Meiji Restoration, the Japanese military modernized their land forces after the German model and their naval forces after the British Royal Navy.

A massive Russian soldier taken prisoner by diminutive Japanese troops during the Russo-Japanese War. The artist entitled this illustration "Brobdingnag and Lilliput" after the fictitious islands inhabited by giants and tiny people in Jonathan Swift's *Gulliver's Travels*.

navy did not extend to its generals and soldiers. The Japanese armies swept through Korea and Manchuria and captured Port Arthur (Lushun). James Creelman, the American war correspondent for Joseph Pulitzer's *The World*, witnessed the massacre. He reported: "The defenceless and unarmed inhabitants were butchered in their houses and their bodies unspeakably mutilated. There was an unrestrained reign of murder which continued for three days." It was an ominous forerunner of things to come.

The Sino-Japanese War (1894–5) completely upset the balance of power in the region. Nobody, apart from the Japanese, thought that Japan could defeat China. The predatory Western nations took full advantage of China's recently exposed weakness, at the same time forcing Japan to give up most of the territory it had captured.

Russia obtained a lease on the Liaodong Peninsula. It fortified Port Arthur and started building the terminus of a railway from Dairen (Dalian) to Moscow, which was designed to transport the massive Russian armies overland to China. The British saw this as an extension of the Great Game, with China replacing India as the ultimate target for invasion. By securing a lease on the naval base at Weihaiwei, Britain hoped to contain the situation. The German Kaiser Wilhelm II was determined to build an overseas empire to rival those of the British and French. He used the old excuse of the murder of two missionaries to secure Tsingtao (Qingdao), where he could build his own naval base. The scramble for concessions had begun.

If the West was alarmed by Japan's victory, China was absolutely shattered. The humiliation of being defeated by a small Asian nation led to the formation of the Reform Movement. A group of scholar-officials led by Kang Yu-wei (Kang Youwei) managed to gain the confidence of Emperor Kuang Hsu (Guangxu), who had just come of age. During what became known as "The Hundred Days," the emperor issued a number of edicts designed to modernize and democratize China.

His aunt, the Empress Dowager Tzu Hsi, who had virtually ruled China as regent for forty-seven years, staged a coup and imprisoned the emperor for the rest of his life. She was supported by Yuan Shih-kai (Yuan Shikai), who was just about the only Chinese general who had emerged from the Sino-Japanese War with any credit. History is littered with autocrats who have held on to power too long. They tend to lose touch with reality. The empress dowager is an extreme example. During the Boxer Rebellion, she declared war on the eleven most powerful nations in the world. The outcome was inevitable.

Unlike Lord Elgin, who burnt down the Summer Palace in an exercise of bloodless retribution, the often undisciplined allied forces of the avenging armies had no such qualms, and looting got completely out of hand. The worst offenders were not the soldiers, but the survivors of the siege, who knew the value of the treasures that they looted and where they were hidden. Foreign residents, like B. L. Putnam Weale, looted only in the Russian zone where they were safe from being arrested by the British or American authorities. There is a fine line between the legitimate spoils of war and uncontrolled looting which has never been defined, but for the survivors of the siege it was an unholy mixture of greed and vengeance.

*Far left*: Sun Yat-sen, the first president of China, was a dedicated revolutionary. He is revered as the "Father of the Nation" in China.

*Left*: Yuan Shih-kai (Yuan Shikai) became the second president of China after the overthrow of the Ching dynasty. His attempt to make himself emperor failed.

*Below*: Manchurian bandits attacking Russian officials during the Russo-Japanese War.

*Opposite*: For almost 50 years the Empress Dowager Tzu Hsi was the *de facto* ruler of China. Her desire to retain power at any cost brought about the fall of the Ching dynasty. This picture was taken in 1903 during her twilight years.

The victorious nations grabbed land, mining and railway concessions. Russia virtually took over Manchuria and Korea. This was too much for Japan who launched a pre-emptive strike and sank most of the Russian fleet at Port Arthur. Russian reinforcements were unable to reach Manchuria in large numbers because of the Siberian winter. The Russian commander of Port Arthur lacked the tenacity of the defenders of the legations of Peking (Beijing). He surrendered without consulting his officers, although he still had the means to hold out for several more months. The final humiliation was the sinking of the Russian Baltic Fleet at the Battle of Tsushima. Japan suffered 85,000 casualties in the war, which for a country of 45 million would have been unsustainable if the war had continued. Japan's defeat of Russia and China eventually led to the downfall of both tsar and emperor in the decade that followed.

After the Boxer Rebellion, the allies treated the empress dowager more as an impotent old curiosity than anything else. The wives of diplomats took tea with her and she allowed her portrait to be painted by an American lady. However, the Machiavellian old dragon empress was still active. She persuaded the Grand Council to accept Pu Yi (Puyi) as the heir to the unfortunate Kuang Hsu, who was still imprisoned. The emperor died mysteriously in 1908, on the day before the empress dowager herself passed away. He was almost certainly murdered.

In mediaeval Europe, the succession of a child monarch was looked upon as a disaster because it was the frequent cause of civil wars. China had three successive child emperors. Pu Yi was only three years old when the dragon empress died. The regent, Prince Chun, and a cartel of nobles attempted to re-establish the power of the Manchus over their Chinese subjects. They failed. There was a revolution on 10 November 1911, and Sun Yat-sen became the first president of China, with the intention of establishing a modern republic ruled by Han Chinese.

He was soon replaced by Yuan Shih-kai, who had the strongest army in China. But Yuan was unable to control the military governors of the provinces of the empire. This unpopular autocrat tried and failed to make himself emperor. By the time of his death in 1916, China had disintegrated into opposing military cliques. This was the beginning of the warlord period. Civil war raged through China for the next forty years. Japan invaded in the 1930s, and China was torn apart until peace came at last with the establishment of the People's Republic of China by Mao Tse-tung (Mao Zedong) in 1949.

# Weihaiwei: The Scramble for Concessions

For over half a century, Britain, France and Russia were the dominant foreign powers in China. The Sino-Japanese War (1894–5) triggered off the "Scramble for Concessions." Japan forced China to cede Taiwan (Formosa) and the Liaodong Peninsula in Manchuria. This was too much for Russia, France and Germany, who persuaded Japan to return Liaodong to China.

The "cutting up of the melon" began. The convenient murder of two German missionaries provided Kaiser Wilhelm II with the excuse to annex Tsingtao (Qingdao). Russia bribed Li Hung-chang to arrange for them to acquire Liaodong with its naval base at Port Arthur. To retain the balance of power, Britain leased Weihaiwei "for as long as Russia remains in Port Arthur" and also took over the New Territories in Hong Kong at the same time.

Hong Kong and Weihaiwei were geographically similar. They were about the same size. Each had a strategic island and contained a walled city which, in theory, retained Chinese sovereignty. Unlike Hong Kong, Weihaiwei was never an emporium of trade in spite of its magnificent harbor. Between the two world wars it was a fashionable holiday resort for expatriates. The two great civil commissioners, Sir James Stewart Lockhart and Sir Reginald Johnston, were both considerable Chinese scholars. Johnston also achieved fame as the tutor of the last emperor, Pu Yi, before becoming Weihaiwei's last commissioner.

The two men created a pragmatic system of Chinese and British law to rule Weihaiwei that actually worked. When Lockhart retired, he was presented with a bowl of crystal clear water by the Chinese as a symbol of the purity of his administration. Ironically, a street called Lockhart Road in the red-light district of Hong Kong, Wanchai, is named after him.

Weihaiwei was known as the "Cinderella of the British Empire." It became a fashionable holiday resort for expatriates during the turbulent years following the collapse of the Ching dynasty. The British agreed to return Weihaiwei to China at the Washington Conference, but when the time came, the "Christian General" Feng Yu-hsiang (Feng Yuxiang) captured Peking and there was no Chinese government to return it to. Weihaiwei was eventually returned to China in 1930.

This modest little bungalow was called Government House where the commissioner, who ruled the territory, lived. It was located in Port Edward, on the mainland west of the city of Weihaiwei (Weihai), which was under Chinese administration.

*Left*: Sir Reginald Johnston, the last British commissioner of Weihaiwei, attending a garden party in the 1920s. The number of foreign residents in the territory during the British administration was very small, seldom more than a couple of hundred.

*Below*: Seymour Street on Liukung (Liugong) Island was named after Admiral Sir Edward Seymour. In the background can be seen Admiral Ting's headquarters where he committed suicide after surrendering to the Japanese during the Sino-Japanese War.

*Left*: A panorama of the walled city of Weihaiwei in 1901. The city was outside British jurisdiction. Most foreigners lived on Liukung Island which can be seen in the background. The main naval base and barracks were on the island.

*Below*: The Royal Navy's China Fleet at anchor at Weihaiwei on an annual visit in the 1920s. Unlike the Russians at Port Arthur and Germans at Tsingtao, the British did not transform the port into a massive naval base.

# Mortimer Menpes: Whistler's Disciple

Mortimer Menpes lived in the golden age of book illustration. Although he was overshadowed by giants like William Morris, Edmund Dulac and Arthur Rackham, his etchings are much admired by collectors of prints.

Born in Australia, he had already established himself as a printmaker in London when he met James McNeill Whistler, the great American artist. Menpes had a studio in Fulham, where he had set up an etching press. He invited Whistler to use his studio. Whistler, who was what Australians call a bludger and romantics call a bohemian, took full advantage of the offer. For seven years the two artists worked closely together. Menpes even made an etching of Whistler's mother—not a copy of Whistler's masterpiece, but of the old lady herself. Both Whistler and Menpes originally made their names as artists through etching. Whistler loved the medium: "Let us cleanse ourselves, Menpes. Let us print an etching."

In 1887, Menpes went to Japan. This resulted in a successful exhibition. Whistler, whose painting was influenced by Japanese woodblock prints, had a fit of jealousy. Menpes wrote: "Directly I returned from Japan and the Master left me, the Followers also left in a body—I was an outcast. I took up my brush, began my solitary artistic life, and tried to make a success." In 1909, he published a book of his paintings of China.

Some art historians contemptuously dismiss Menpes as "Whistler's studio assistant." The Master, in his biography, *The Gentle Art of Making Enemies*, had something to say about such art critics: "I hold that none but an artist can be a competent critic." In spite of their quarrel, there is plenty of evidence that Whistler admired Menpes's skills as a printmaker.

The Master was infamous for his viciousness towards former buddies. Menpes got off rather lightly. Whistler's friendship with his fellow artists Alphonse Legros and Seymour Haden ended violently! He punched Legros in the head and knocked Haden through a plate-glass window.

*Above*: James Whistler's mother. Mortimer Menpes made this etching about ten years after Whistler painted his original masterpiece. The old lady was in her late seventies when the Australian artist made this print soon after he first met Whistler.

*Opposite*: A quiet canal. China has the most sophisticated canal system ever created. The Grand Canal is the longest in the world. Menpes was fascinated by canals. He had illustrated a book on Venice.

*Far left*: An old scholar. The most revered members of the Chinese establishment were the literati. Because of the importance of agriculture in China, farmers were second on the social scale. Craftsmen came third and businessmen were a dismal fourth.

*Left*: A young scholar. It was the ambition of every student to pass the civil service examination. A successful scholar, no matter how humble, was allowed to wear a gold button on the top of his hat. These examinations were the road to a successful career.

*Above*: Western artists visiting China seem to have been impelled to produce at least one junk seascape. This painting, "Junks at Eventide," was probably inspired by Whistler's famous "Thames Set" of etchings rather than by the craft themselves.

*Right*: An ancient grandfather. Old people were highly respected in Chinese society largely due to the teachings of Confucius, where filial piety and obedience to elders were paramount factors.

*Far right*: During the Ching dynasty, young Han Chinese girls did not normally wear their hair loose. It was generally plaited into a queue until marriage when it was put up in elaborate and exotic coiffures.

*Opposite*: Watching a game of chess. A Chinese chess piece is a simple disk like a draught with a character painted on it for identification. The rules as well as the pieces are very different from the Western versions.

THE END OF EMPIRE AND THE NEW REPUBLIC 165

# Tzu Hsi: The Dragon Empress

For almost fifty years until her death in 1908, the Empress Dowager Tzu Hsi was the *de facto* ruler of China. She was the daughter of a Manchu bannerman. In 1852, at the age of sixteen, she became a concubine fifth rank to the Emperor Hsien Feng (Xianfeng).

She was extremely shrewd and made friends with the Empress Niuhuru (Ci An). She also became a favorite of the powerful palace eunuchs. In 1856, she gave birth to the emperor's only son, Tung Chih (Tongzhi).

As the foreign armies advanced on Peking during the Arrow War, the imperial court fled to Jehol where the emperor died in 1861. A cartel of mandarins and princes seized power. However, the two empresses and Prince Kung (Gong), the emperor's brother, staged a coup. Tzu Hsi and Niuhuru became dowager empresses of China. Tung Chih was only six years old, so the empresses and Prince Kung became regents. A power struggle soon developed between Tzu Hsi and Prince Kung.

As an adolescent, the Emperor Tung Chih, encouraged by the palace eunuchs, became more interested in visiting brothels than in affairs of state and he died of the pox.

Tzu Hsi conspired successfully to get her younger sister's four-year-old son, Kuang Hsu (Guangxu), proclaimed emperor. Prince Kung was forced to retire and Tzu Hsi became sole regent.

China's weakness was its mediaeval navy. Prince Kung and Li Hung-chang had attempted to build up a viable naval force, but Tzu Hsi purloined the funds and spent them building a new Summer Palace, near to the old one, the Yuanmingyuan, where she cynically constructed a beautiful marble boat on a palace lake.

During the Sino-Japanese War, the Chinese imperial fleet was destroyed. The Chinese had some fine warships but insufficient ammunition. The humiliating defeat by a smaller Asian power was largely responsible for the formation of Kang Yu-wei's (Kang Youwei's) Reform Movement.

In 1898, the Emperor Kuang Hsu, who had come of age, appointed Kang as his secretary. They proposed a number of reforms during a period known as "The Hundred Days." This infuriated the dragon empress who staged another coup; she imprisoned Kuang Hsu and ruled China until her death in 1908.

The Empress Tzu Hsi surrounded by her court ladies. Before she imprisoned the Emperor Kuang Hsu, she forced him to marry her niece, the Empress Lung Yu (Longyu), seen here on the right of the picture.

*Far left*: Prince Kung was the younger brother of the Emperor Hsien Feng. He became co-regent with Tzu Hsi and the Empress Niuhuru after their coup. In 1884, the dragon empress forced Prince Kung to retire from public office.

*Left*: A formal portrait of the dragon empress. She was the mother of the only son of the Emperor Hsien Feng. Shortly after the emperor died in 1861, she seized power and ruled China until her death in 1908.

*Below*: The notorious Marble Boat was financed through the embezzlement of navy funds by the dragon empress. This beautiful folly has long been regarded as a symbol of corrupt Manchu imperialism. It can still be seen at Lake Kunming in the Summer Palace.

*Above*: The Potala at Jehol (Chengde). The Emperor Hsien Feng died at Jehol, where he had taken refuge during the Arrow War. A cartel of Manchu princes tried to detain Tzu Hsi and the young emperor, but they escaped to Peking.

*Left*: The Nine Dragon Spirit Screen at the Winter Palace in Peking. Each dragon on this protective screen is different and has a special symbolic significance. The five-clawed dragon was the emblem of the emperor, who sat on the Dragon Throne.

*Opposite*: A view of the New Summer Palace (Yiheyuan). In the center stands the Buddha Fragrance Pagoda (Xianfoge) on a 68-foot stone platform. It was damaged during the Arrow War and was rebuilt by the dragon empress in the late nineteenth century.

# The Boxer Rebellion: The Siege of the Legations

The Society of Righteous and Harmonious Fists, popularly known as the Boxers, was an anti-foreign, anti-Christian secret society manipulated by xenophobic imperial officials infuriated by the "Scramble for Concessions."

The Boxers began slaughtering missionaries in the provinces. In 1900, they entered Peking and burnt down the racecourse. Two days later, they murdered the chancellor of the Japanese legation. After the German minister was shot by an imperial soldier, it became obvious that the Ching government was involved. Soon attacks on the legations began. The siege at Peking went on for two months.

Almost daily, imperial Ching bannermen and the Boxers attacked the legations. The British Minister, Sir Claude MacDonald, a former captain in the Highland Light Infantry, organized the defense with a force of under 400 trained soldiers and marines from eight different countries and a similar number of volunteers. An old cannon from the Arrow War, unearthed and repaired, fired bags of nails at the enemy. Sandbags of "satin brocades" were made by the women and "butterfly-colored" barricades were constructed by a missionary, a former engineer.

Food was a problem although, ironically, there was an abundance of champagne and cigars. Any animal that could be eaten was; generally, mules were preferred to polo ponies. The pilfering of supplies almost became a sport. The best chicken thief was the Dutch plenipotentiary who targeted the Russian minister's poultry. The worst off were the 2,000 Chinese Christians who had sought refuge in the legations. The relief force arrived, but the carefully planned allied assault on the city walls began in chaos because the Russians attacked not only ahead of zero hour, but the wrong gate. This left the Americans with a hotly defended 30-foot wall to climb. Meanwhile, General Gaselee's Sikhs poured into the city through the unguarded gate of a smelly sewer, euphemistically called the Imperial Drainage Canal.

This dramatic painting of a Boxer was reproduced in the *Illustrated London News* during the siege. It was not until the Boxers burnt down Peking Racecourse that the British Minister, Sir Claude MacDonald, telegraphed the Royal Navy for help.

*Above*: Morrison in the Chinese costume that he wore during his remarkable journey from Shanghai to Rangoon in 1894. On arriving at the Burmese border, he discarded his Chinese dress in favor of "the aesthetic garments of the Australian bush."

*Far left*: Sir Edmund Backhouse's discredited book, *China Under the Empress Dowager*, contained some beautiful photographs, including this one of Emperor Pu Yi's cousin and playmate, Pu Ju, a grandson of Prince Kung.

*Left*: Tsai Ying, pictured here with his son, was a cousin of the imprisoned Emperor Kuang Hsu. Tsai Ying's pro-Boxer activities led to his being cashiered by the dragon empress as a sop to the allied armies after they had relieved the legations.

# Port Arthur: The Russian Concession in Manchuria

During the "Scramble for Concessions" in 1898, the Russians obtained the lease of the Liaodong Peninsula which had remained in the hands of the Japanese after the Sino-Japanese War. The whole territory was known as Port Arthur. It contained a strategic naval base, Port Arthur (Lushun), and Dairen (Dalian), a tiny fishing village. Port Arthur was named after Captain William Arthur whose ship, HMS *Algerine*, anchored there in 1860.

Previously, the vast Russian empire was without a warm-water naval base. They made Port Arthur a formidable fortress. Dairen was to be the terminus of a railway stretching from Moscow to Manchuria. The British writer B. L. Putnam Weale described it in 1903: "Every species of architecture abounded, from the Swiss cottage to quaint buildings faced with Italian loggias, from Elizabethan houses to strange fluted hybrids."

Putnam Weale spent an alcoholic day at the races, noting: "In Port Arthur everybody backs the favourite, and the favourite always wins." The social life was liquid. "In Manchuria you do not say in the manner of an Englishman, 'Have a drink,' you simply drink, and then wait for the next bottle to be opened."

The Japanese resented Russia occupying Port Arthur. In 1904, Admiral Togo launched a pre-emptive night attack on the Russian fleet. He sank three battleships and four cruisers and blockaded the port. Tsar Nicholas II reacted by sending his Baltic Fleet from Europe to China. On the way, a few miles off the English coast, it shelled a harmless British fishing fleet. Admiral Rozhestvensky, in a fit of paranoia, thought he was being attacked by Japanese torpedo boats and sank a fishing trawler.

By the time the Baltic Fleet arrived in Chinese waters, the Japanese had already captured Port Arthur. Admiral Togo sank most of Rozhestvensky's fleet at the Battle of Tsushima in 1905.

The impact of the Russo-Japanese War was incalculable. It was the first defeat of a massive Western power by Asian forces since the days of Attila the Hun, fourteen centuries earlier. The capture of Port Arthur and the devastating destruction of the Russian fleet shocked the world.

*Left*: The Russian attack on a British fishing fleet in the North Sea almost provoked a war. Admiral Rozhestvensky inexplicably mistook the British trawlers for Japanese torpedo boats. Two British fishermen were killed when the Hull trawler *Crane* was sunk.

*Opposite below*: Tsar Nicholas II sent the Russian Baltic Fleet halfway around the world to relieve Port Arthur. After Port Arthur fell to the Japanese, the fleet attempted to reach Vladivostok, but was sunk by Admiral Togo at the Battle of Tsushima in 1905.

*Far left*: Port Arthur was named after Lieutenant-Commander William Arthur, the captain of HMS *Algerine*, after two Royal Navy survey ships found the *Algerine* anchored in a remote Manchurian bay during a hydrographic survey of the Yellow Sea in 1860.

*Left*: A Japanese soldier stands triumphantly on the ruins of Niri-usan Fort, Port Arthur. It was the strongest fort in the northern siege line. The rubble in the foreground was caused by Japanese sappers exploding several tons of dynamite under the fort.

# Life before Television in Expatriate China

It is difficult in the twenty-first century to imagine how a large expatriate family entertained itself in China a hundred years ago. The popular modern formula of nuking a heap of frozen food in the microwave and plonking the kids in front of the television was, of course, technologically impossible in those days.

Keeping children amused in the evening required more effort. Music was important and family concerts were popular. Those who could afford it bought a piano, but not all children are musical, and tone-deaf children specialized in recitations. Precocious infants lisped their way through "Humpty Dumpty" while sentimental and patriotic ballads were popular with teenagers.

Every child had to have a party piece. *Gamages Christmas Bazaar Catalogue* is crowded with advertisements of items for home entertainment, ranging from cabinets of conjuring tricks to instruments of torture, such as rubber bagpipes.

For the totally untalented, there was the magic lantern. Ancient slide shows were less agonizing to watch than most modern home videos because the pictures were taken by professional photographers.

The Dutch claim that the magic lantern was invented by Christiaan Huygens around 1660. His projector was a lantern, a candle and a lens, and his slides were hand-painted on glass. The screen was a white wall. By Edwardian times, the projector had become more sophisticated to the extent that it could be focused and glass slides with colored printed transfers or photographs were used.

Stereoscopes were also popular. They produced a three-dimensional image. Like spectacles, they had two lenses. You slid a card, which had two images printed on it side-by-side, towards you until you went almost cross-eyed, and the photographs merged by magic into a single three-dimensional picture.

Some of China's greatest early photographers made stereos and their photographs were frequently reproduced on lantern slides. These were often very crudely hand-colored. In spite of this, they are popular collectables.

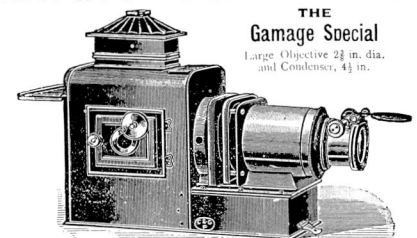
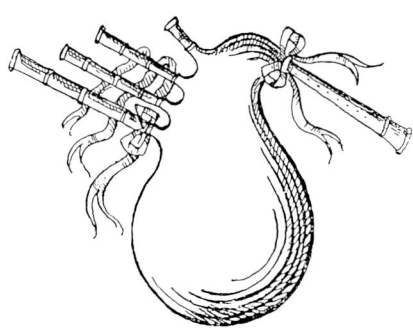

Arthur Gamage called his department store "The People's Emporium." His cut-price 900-page mail order *Gamages Christmas Bazaar Catalogue*, was a "must" for every expatriate amateur entertainer. Gamage sold everything from accordions to zonophones. A set of rubber bagpipes posted in London on 12 November would arrive in Shanghai just in time to ruin a family Christmas.

*Above:* A stereoscope of the Canton River taken during the occupation of the city in the Arrow War. The houses on the left were demolished after they had been used by Chinese snipers. Honan Island can be seen in the background.

*Below:* "At 'Chow'—breakfast—in China." This comes from a 100-card set of stereoscopes published by Underwood & Underwood. It was photographed by James Ricalton in 1900. He is best known for developing the bamboo filaments used in Thomas Edison's electric lamps.

THE END OF EMPIRE AND THE NEW REPUBLIC 179

*Left*: A typical tourist lantern slide of a Chinese using chopsticks. Lantern slides were made of glass and hand-colored. They were sandwiched between two pieces of clear glass. The coloring tended to be rather crude. This lantern slide is a glorious exception.

*Below*: A post-revolution lantern slide of a family group dressed in their best clothes. The mother's feet are not bound and the father wears a foreign trilby hat. The boys have post-Manchu haircuts. There is a spittoon placed strategically in the foreground.

*Opposite above*: A lantern slide showing the elaborate variety of coiffures of a group of young girls. The hairstyles of baby boys were also exotic. Adolescent boys had to shave their foreheads and wear the hated Manchu queue as a symbol of subjection to their conquerors.

*Far left*: Wearing the *cangue* was a punishment in imperial China for minor offences. The heavy wooden collar was designed to prevent criminals from feeding themselves. This is a typical example of a famous photograph being used as a lantern slide.

*Left*: A formal studio portrait of a couple of expatriate boys dressed up in sailor suits. Children like this were expected to perform their party piece as a contribution to family entertainment. Nowadays, Batman and Spiderman costumes are preferred to sailor suits.

# A Touch of Satire in Ching China

Shanghai between the turn of the century and World War I was run by foreign businessmen for the benefit of foreign businessmen. Unfortunately, businessmen seldom make good politicians because they fail to realize that politics is about people. The Shanghai satirist Jay Denby may have had this old saying in mind when he wrote: "The Municipal Council is composed of men who appear to be intimately acquainted with every wickedness of which the human mind is capable; for they guard against lawlessness with an ingenuity only possible to those of ripe experience."

The councilors were almost exclusively taipans from the leading foreign firms. Denby describes a typical taipan: "A taipan, let me explain, is a red-faced man (the redder the face, the taipanner the taipan) who has either sufficient brains or bluff to make others work for him and yet retain the kudos and bulk of the spoil for himself."

Denby tried to unravel the social system in Shanghai. He interviewed a society lady: "She explained that Society proper in Shanghai consisted of herself and another lady, who had gone home for the hot weather." And added, "In the course of five days I learned of sixty-four other cliques, mainly consisting of only one family, or at the most two, not one of whom knows the others officially."

There was even a humorous weekly, *The Eastern Sketch*, which was edited by the cartoonist H. W. G. Hayter, who illustrated Denby's book, *Letters from China*. The best-known satirist was B. L. Putnam Weale, whose *Indiscreet Letters from Peking* is sometimes mistaken for a serious history of the siege at Peking because the author was one of the besieged.

Putnam Weale's main target for attack was Sir Claude MacDonald, who had tried to have him arrested for looting after the siege. Sir Claude was a gift for any journalist with a grudge. Morrison of Peking described him as the "type of military officer rolled out a mile at a time and then lopped off in six foot lengths."

*Above*: H. W. G. Hayter was the owner, editor and principal cartoonist of *The Eastern Sketch* which was published every Sunday in Shanghai and sold at 30 cents a copy.

*Left and center*: The dress sense of sing-song girls is reflected by the sartorial combination of deerstalker hat, mandarin jacket, tartan trews and "Golden Lilies." These cartoons appeared in Jay Denby's book, *Letters from China*.

Sir Claude MacDonald's enormous waxed moustache made him a caricaturist's dream. His critics reviled him as a British army stereotype and gave him little credit for his successful defense of the legations.

An *Eastern Sketch* reprint of a Chinese cartoon. The caption reads: "Casting pearls before swine, or Sinice, playing the harp to a cow. The characters translated mean 'The Constitutional Government harp.' The cow doubtless represents the official classes."

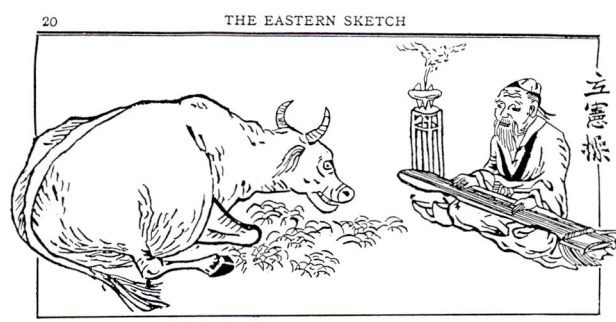

*Above*: Kuo Sung-tao was the first Chinese ambassador to Britain. It was a social triumph for his picture to appear in *Vanity Fair*. Sir Leslie Ward, who used the pseudonym "Spy", was the artist. The cartoon appeared in his "Statesmen" series.

*Left*: A 1907 cover of *The Eastern Sketch* featuring a cartoon by Hayter. The horseman's coiffure incorporates a compulsory Manchu haircut crowned with a startling mohawk punk creation. In those days, it was considered improper for Chinese ladies to ride astride.

# The Double Tenth 1911 and the Fall of the House of Ching

The death of the Empress Dowager Tzu Hsi in 1908 heralded the end of the Chinese empire. The Emperor Kuang Hsu died mysteriously the day before the empress, leaving the unfortunate myopic child Pu Yi to ascend the Dragon Throne at the age of three.

The new regent, Prince Chun, made some reforms, but it soon became clear that his main objective was to re-establish the Manchus as the supreme military power in the empire. He dismissed General Yuan Shih-kai, who had been the empress dowager's most powerful Chinese supporter and was extremely ambitious.

In April 1911, Prince Chun formed a thirteen-man cabinet as a token step towards constitutional monarchy. It consisted of nine Manchus and only four Han Chinese. A few days later, there was a badly organized Chinese rebellion at Canton that failed.

Sun Yat-sen's republicans planned another uprising. A bomb exploded accidentally in Wuchang in October, which triggered off the rebellion prematurely. The local government army commander, Li Yuan-hung (Li Yuan-hong), was persuaded at gunpoint to lead the revolution, which spread quickly over seventeen provinces of China.

The Manchu administration hastily recalled Yuan Shih-kai to put down the revolution. Yuan, a great opportunist, changed sides. Sun Yat-sen arrived in Shanghai on Christmas Day and was elected the provisional president of China on 1 January 1912, and China became a republic.

Sun Yat-sen had offered to step down as president once the emperor had abdicated. The treacherous Yuan Shih-kai, who controlled by far the most powerful army in China, forced the Manchu nobles to agree. Sun Yat-sen resigned and Yuan Shih-kai formed a new republican government with Sun Yat-sen as the director of railways. Yuan later tried to make himself the emperor of China … and failed. When he died in 1916, China had disintegrated into factions dominated by ambitious generals. The warlord era had begun.

Sun Yat-sen achieved his initial objectives, which were to rid China of the foreign Manchu emperors and establish a republic. The Tenth of October is known as the "Double Tenth" in Taiwan and Sun Yat-sen throughout China as "The Father of the Nation."

*Left*: The accidental explosion of a bomb brought forward plans for an uprising at Wuchang. On 10 October 1911, after the police began making arrests, the revolutionaries struck. The following day the city, pictured here, was in rebel hands.

*Opposite*: The last emperor of China, Pu Yi, ascended the dragon throne at the age of three. He spent most of his unhappy life as a pawn or prisoner of the powerful. He died in 1967, having spent his last years as a humble gardener.

*Right*: Hankow's (Hankou's) main river gateway where the revolutionists made their last stand. Hangkow, which had fallen to the revolutionists early in the rebellion, was recaptured in November 1911 by the Manchu imperialists, who then burnt the city.

*Below*: The Provincial Assembly Hall at Wuchang. General Li Yuan-hung, the reluctant leader of the Wuchang uprising, used this magnificent building as his military headquarters in the early days of the revolution.

*Left*: Dr Sun Yat-sen led a number of rebellions against the foreign Manchu government. He was the president of the Revolutionary Alliance (Tongmenghui) at the time of the Wuchang uprising in 1911, and consequently became the first president of China.

*Below left*: Yuan Shih-kai, the second president of China. Yuan controlled the loyalty of the only effective army in China. He had been dismissed by the regent, Prince Chun, but after he was recalled to put down the revolution, he changed sides.

*Left*: Li Yuan-hung, the third president of China. Sun Yat-sen was abroad when the Wuchang uprising erupted prematurely. The conspirators persuaded Li Yuan-hung, a popular local officer, at gunpoint to lead the revolution. He agreed.

# A Camel in the Chinese Customs Service

Drink and sport were the two most popular methods used by expatriates to protect themselves from tropical diseases. Paul King was a fitness fanatic and survived forty-seven years in the Chinese Imperial Customs Service. Unfortunately, his chief, Sir Robert Hart, had an eccentric loathing for all forms of physical exercise to the extent that he would not allow his son to play cricket, rugby, tennis, or any other sport, at school.

King's first posting was Swatow (Shantou). The fear of catching cholera was so strong that expatriates lived off "metallic meals," mainly tinned sausages. King supplemented this dreary diet by shooting anything edible that moved. Alcohol was considered a preventive medicine and he joined the Jambarree Club, which was famed on the China coast for its hard drinking.

There were numerous sporting clubs in cities like Shanghai and Tientsin (Tianjin), but some Treaty Ports did not even have a tennis court. King was a great improviser. When the Yangtze flooded at Kiukiang (Jiujiang), it created a vast lake and he immediately formed a sailing club; at Ichang (Yichang) he used the dry river bed of the Yangtze as a golf course. If there was not a gym, he founded one. A formidable boxer and fencer, he was taught *kendo* by a Japanese police inspector in Shanghai.

As "a self-convicted athlete," he was not a favorite of Sir Robert and because of his love of sport promotion was slow. During an official dinner, Sir Robert asked King: "And pray, how do you invest your money?" King replied bitterly, "In boots and shoes for my family." King wrote, "The great man was not amused" and afterwards promotion became even slower.

Sir Robert Hart's niece wrote a sickly, sycophantic biography of the great man. Paul King's book, *In the Chinese Customs Service*, was designed to put the record straight. He explains his motivation in "revealing all" by quoting an old Arabian saying: "The camel driver has his opinions—and the camel also has his!"

*Above*: Sir Robert Hart and his subordinate Paul King did not get on: "He was a declared enemy of athletics, or games of a like tendency, and never indulged in any manly sport," wrote fitness fanatic King, "and he had no liking for club life."

*Opposite*: The camel was the beast of burden of northern China. For centuries these creatures carried enormous loads from the lonely steppes of Outer Mongolia, and beyond, along the ancient caravan routes to Peking, covering around 20 miles a day.

*Left*: Paul King spent forty-seven years in the Chinese Customs Service, in ten different treaty ports. His autobiography is rich in stories of expatriate life.

*Right*: When the Kiukiang Bund was flooded in 1879, the indomitable King started a sailing club.

*Opposite below*: The Customs House at Wuchow (Wuzhou), about 180 miles upstream from Canton (Guangzhou) in Kwangsi (Guangxi) province. It became a treaty port in 1897. It was a distribution center for trade with the inland provinces.

King was fascinated by martial arts. He was taught *kendo* by a Japanese police inspector. In return, he taught the samurai fencing. They sometimes fought mixed bouts, matching either an *épée* or a saber against the two-handed Japanese sword.

# The Maker of Heavenly Trousers

China has always had more than its fair share of expatriate eccentrics, possibly because the only way to stay sane in that country is to become an eccentric. Diplomats are not immune. Daniele Varè, the First Secretary of the Italian Embassy, was born an eccentric. Describing his fellow diplomats, he wrote: "They lived a life of complete detachment from that of the Chinese, in a sort of diplomatic mountain fastness."

His wife Bettina loved exploring exotic places. She insisted on the family becoming vegetarian after seeing a leper leaning up against the carcass of a calf hung outside a butcher's shop. Consequently, Varè declared the equally unhygienic vegetable market out of bounds to Bettina.

Bettina bought a cow to provide milk for their baby and unsuccessfully attempted to milk the animal herself. She mentioned her predicament at an embassy dinner. The Portuguese Minister, who was of Irish descent, solved the problem immediately. "The cow, after a surprised look at Martins O'Connor's decorations and Bettina's diamonds, accepted their ministrations with becoming gratitude."

During World War I, Italy fought on the allied side. When the enemy German Embassy caught fire, the Italian fire engine rushed to the rescue. Varè's gallant firemen, instead of inserting the hose into a well, stuck it into a cesspool and smothered the fire.

Varè had a feeling for China. His novel, *The Maker of Heavenly Trousers*, is about the problems confronting expatriates in China. Unlike in other books on the subject, the inscrutable Chinese always come out on top. It is one of the most delightful books ever written on Peking. His characters include a scholar-journalist and his child bride; their servants, the Five Virtues; a family of insane White Russians; a Mongolian abbot prince who brainwashes a terminally ill millionaire; and the former mistress of Rasputin, the mad monk. The only creature in the book who is remotely normal is Mr Podger, a small Pekinese dog.

His characters seem fantastic, but become quite credible when compared to real people like Backhouse or Baron Ungern-Sternberg, who claimed to be the reincarnation of Genghis Khan.

The Portuguese Minister, Martins O'Connor, teaching Bettina Varè how to milk her cow after she had fired her cowman for watering down the milk. Bettina, who was neurotic about hygiene, had bought the creature to provide milk for her baby.

*Left*: The German Embassy. During World War I, the Italians, who were on the allies' side, kindly put out a fire in the embassy. They possessed the only fire engine in the legations. Unfortunately, they stuck their hose in a cesspool instead of a well.

*Below*: The Legation Quarter in the Tartar City in 1925. After its almost total destruction during the Boxer Rebellion, it was rebuilt on a grand scale. Here diplomats lived in a palatial self-contained foreign ghetto completely cut off from the Chinese population.

*Opposite*: The Lama Temple where the Mongolian abbot prince performed a minor miracle. As if blessing Kuniang, he stretched out his arms "and immediately, on to the tip of the middle finger of each hand, there came a butterfly, and posed itself with closed wings."

*Above*: The Hsi Pien Men Gate at Peking. The Maker of Heavenly Trousers, his child bride Kuniang, and her Pekinese dog Mr Podger, lived in an ancient mansion behind the gate in the southwest corner of the Tartar City.

*Right*: Daniele Varè was the author of *The Maker of Heavenly Trousers*, a classic book about expatriate society in Peking. Varè was appointed First Secretary of the Italian Embassy in 1912. He returned to China as the Italian Minister twelve years later.

*Left*: Many of the incidents in the book and its two sequels, *The Gate of Happy Sparrows* and *The Temple of Costly Experience*, concern the antics of dubious antiques and curio dealers. Like his hero, Varè was an enthusiastic collector of Chinese antiquities and works of art.

THE END OF EMPIRE AND THE NEW REPUBLIC 195

# Chapter 4

# TURBULENCE AND DECADENCE
## (1919–1927)

At the beginning of World War I, the Japanese, who were on the side of the allies, captured the German treaty port of Tsingtao (Qingdao) in Shantung (Shandong) province. They then issued China with Twenty-One Demands which were intended to reduce China to the state of a Japanese protectorate. By declaring war on Germany in 1917, China hoped to regain the German concessions in China.

However, after the war, at the Peace Conference at Versailles, the allies agreed that Japan would be allotted Germany's rights in Shantung. This caused student protests and led to the formation of the May the Fourth Movement, which in turn led to the revival in popularity of the Kuomintang (Guomindang) and also to the foundation of the Chinese Communist Party in Shanghai in 1921.

The United States became alarmed by Japanese expansionism and militarism in the Pacific region. They convened the Washington Conference in 1921, where Japan agreed reluctantly to withdraw its troops from Shantung and the British and French stated that they were prepared to return their concessions of Weihaiwei (Weihai) and Kwanchowan to China. Only the British fully honored the agreement. It was the first international conference to be conducted in English and also the first to which any Chinese government delegation had been invited. Unfortunately, two Chinese delegations turned up, one from the government in Peking (Beijing) and another from Sun Yat-sen's Kuomintang regime in Canton (Guangzhou), which was snubbed by the foreign powers. This led indirectly to Sun Yat-sen employing Soviet Russian advisers.

China was in chaos. Yuan Shih-kai (Yuan Shikai) had died and the parliament which he had dissolved was recalled by his successor, President Li Yuan-hung (Li Yuanhong), but it had little authority. In the north, a number of wars were fought between the Old Marshal Chang Tso-lin (Zhang Zuolin), the Manchurian warlord, and the Chihili (Zhili) clique of Wu Pei-fu (Wu Peifu).

Wu won the first round with the aid of another warlord, the Christian General Feng Yu-hsiang (Feng Yuxiang). Feng later changed sides because it is alleged that he did not approve of Wu's drinking, and in 1924 his army marched into Peking to the rousing hymn of "Onward Christian Soldiers" and took control of the capital. He expelled the Emperor Pu Yi (Puyi) from the Great Within. The Emperor fled to the comparative safety of the treaty port of Tientsin (Tianjin).

Sun Yat-sen, with great difficulty, was able to re-organize the Kuomintang in Canton aided by the Soviet Russian agent Michael Borodin. Sun established the Whampoa Military Academy and made Chiang Kai-shek its first commandant. In 1926, after the death of Sun Yat-sen, Chiang launched the Northern Expedition. He took control of the Chinese municipality at Shanghai with the aid of Tu Yueh-sheng (Du Yuesheng), known as Big-Eared Tu, a notorious gangster and godfather of the Green Gang, the Shanghai mafia. Tu's gangsters slaughtered the Communists and their Kuomintang left-wing allies. Chiang then expelled the Soviet Russian advisers from China and established the Nationalist government's new capital at Nanking (Nanjing).

There were hundreds of warlords and territory was constantly changing hands. In spite of this, some provinces were relatively well governed in what were almost

*Previous page*: This dramatic photograph of the statue of Sun Yat-sen, "The Father of the Nation," was taken in 1937. It stood in the newly completed Shanghai Civic Center which was shelled and destroyed by Japanese warships deployed in the Whangpoo River.

*Right*: A panorama of Canton. The city was the power base of Sun Yat-sen during the warlord period and the headquarters of his Kuomintang. It was from this city that Chiang Kai-shek launched his successful Northern Expedition.

*Opposite below left*: The Old Marshal Chang Tso-lin ruled Manchuria during the warlord period. This former bandit betrayed every alliance in which he was involved. He was assassinated by the Japanese military, who wanted to colonize Manchuria.

impossible circumstances. Yen Hsi-shan (Yan Xishan), who had been appointed military governor of Shansi (Shanxi) by Yuan Shih-kai, ruled the province as an almost independent state, off and on, for thirty-eight years. He was a disciple of Sun Yat-sen and was actually able to implement and complete a ten-year plan during those turbulent years. He was known as the Model Governor.

Modernization was eccentric and often only cosmetic. Yang Sen, the warlord of Chengtu (Chengdu), did not approve of traditional, old-fashioned Chinese gowns so he stationed his soldiers outside the city gates armed with gigantic pairs of shears. His skirt-shortening crusade was not his only contribution to the emancipation of women. He believed that all women should learn to swim. When his wife refused to co-operate, he unceremoniously threw her into the river in front of a crowd of thousands.

To escape from the tyranny of the warlords, millions of Chinese sought refuge in the treaty ports. Shanghai was the principal safe haven. In so doing, they created the great Shanghai Entrepreneur Race, which was the Chinese twentieth-century commercial equivalent of the Vikings without the bloodshed. The Vikings were a mixture of ferocious Scandinavian tribes who conquered Normandy, England, Scotland, Ireland, Sicily, and the odd crusader kingdom. The descendants of this berserker race built the British empire and were the founding fathers of the United States of America. The pioneers of the Shanghainese Entrepreneur Race came from every province in China. By 1935 there were 1,600,154 Chinese living in the safety of foreign concessions in Shanghai, together with 47,482 foreigners. In addition, the population of the Chinese municipality had risen to over two million. Like the descendants of the Vikings, they and their offspring have spread all over the world. Together with today's 16.74 million inhabitants of Shanghai, these expatriate Chinese call themselves Shanghainese.

On the other hand, the foreign residents of Shanghai liked to call themselves Shanghailanders. They were mainly British, Japanese, American, and Russians. The largest concentration of White Russians in China was in Harbin, in northeast China, where the population in the 1920s was equally divided between Russians and Chinese. The city was known for its beautiful Russian Orthodox churches. There were about 350,000 Russians living in Harbin and Manchuria. Many worked along the railway. There were also a few Russian farming villages in the region dating back to the days of the Tsars.

In 1921, the White Russian and Mongolian army of Baron Ungern-Sternberg captured Urga (Hurae), the holy city of Outer Mongolia, where the Chinese were holding the blind Living Buddha prisoner. The Mad Baron, who was surprisingly a Buddhist, rescued the divine lama. After taking the city the White Russian Cossacks massacred thousands of Chinese, Russian Jews, and Bolsheviks. A few days later, they destroyed two Chinese armies which had been sent against them. The Mad Baron took no prisoners. He attempted to invade Russia, but after some early successes, his troops mutinied and he was captured and executed by the Bolsheviks. The Soviets invaded Mongolia. In the words of the historian Peter Hopkirk, "Baron Ungern-Sternberg had made it easy for the Russians. Mongolia had been handed to Lenin on a plate."

*Above*: The Christian General Feng Yu-hsiang baptized whole battalions of his troops with a fire hose. He despised the excesses of the other warlords. Feng's puritanical moral principles did not deter him from double-crossing his allies frequently.

TURBULENCE AND DECADENCE 199

*Left*: Baron Ungern-Sternberg was a Buddhist White Russian general who captured much of Outer Mongolia after the Russian Revolution. He claimed to be descended from Attila the Hun. The Mad Baron's army of Cossacks and Mongolians was defeated by Soviet Russia.

*Right*: President Li Yuan-hung attempted to reintroduce parliamentary democracy to China, but the power struggle between the military cliques, warlords, breakaway provinces and conflicting political philosophies destroyed all hope of democracy surviving.

Japanese expansionism began with the Sino-Japanese War (1894–5) when they annexed Taiwan and turned Korea into a satellite state. In the Russo-Japanese War (1904–5), they had captured Port Arthur (Lushun) and the Liaodong Peninsula. During World War I, they had occupied Tsingtao and attempted to colonize Shantung.

Their plans were temporarily frustrated by the Washington Conference. With command of the naval bases of Tsingtao and Port Arthur and armies in Korea, Japan's first objective was the conquest of Manchuria, which they achieved in the next decade. Meanwhile, the Japanese population in China and Korea overtook that of all other foreign nationals. The main difference between the Japanese and the foreign nationals was that they were aggressive colonial settlers rather than businessmen or crusading missionaries.

To enter Shanghai, you did not need a passport or even an established nationality. There were thousands of displaced persons in Europe who had lost their nationality after World War I. Some were solid bourgeois, but others were villains. Among them was Trebitsch Lincoln, a former British Member of Parliament who had also been a German spy during the war. Banned from British and American territories and later Germany after being involved in the Kapp Putsch, he slipped into Shanghai in 1927 on a false passport and lived under the pseudonym of Abbot Chao Kung. He spent his time ripping off rich, gullible European Buddhists.

Thousands of fortune-hunting foreigners poured into China. There was panic after Chiang Kai-shek's armies forced the British to give up their treaty port of Hankow (Hankou) during his Northern Expedition in 1927, but the Shanghailanders and other foreigners in the treaty ports lived like there was no tomorrow. Many made vast fortunes which they squandered in the wild nightclubs of Shanghai and Tientsin. The Roaring Twenties hit these cities of sin like a tornado. They were the Sodom and Gomorrah of the East. To quote a tour guide on Shanghai: "When the sun goes in and the lights come out Shanghai becomes another City, the City of Blazing Night, a night life Haroun-al-Raschid never knew, with tales Scheherezade never told the uxoricidal Sultan Shahriyar." Travel books like this attracted the world's idle rich, who arrived by the thousands in the great ocean-going luxury liners to enjoy the fun. The great Victorian poet Robert Browning could have been describing Shanghai before World War II when he wrote: "What of soul was left, I wonder, when the kissing had to stop?"

*Opposite*: Shanghai was known as the "City of Blazing Night." The Sincere Department Store, lit up for its winter sale, was in Nanking Road, the Bond Street cum Fifth Avenue of Shanghai, famous for its fabulous department stores and fashionable shops.

200 CHINA ILLUSTRATED

# The Grandeur of the Three Gorges

The Three Gorges on the upper reaches of the Yangtze River were one of the great natural wonders of the world. In 1919, Sun Yat-sen conceived a plan to harness the turbulent waters of the Yangtze by building the biggest dam in the world. Work eventually began on the dam in 1993. The scheme, which was designed specifically to prevent flooding, will ironically create a vast reservoir that will submerge 13 cities, 114 towns, numerous villages and thousands of archaeological sites.

In the 1920s, Donald Mennie published a book of photographs of the river from Chungking (Chongqing) to Ichang (Yichang). A contemporary of Mennie's, Charles Drage, described Chungking as a "riot of gaily tiled, fantastically curved roofs above grey battlemented walls, from which endless flights of white steps ran down to the river far below." That was when it had a population at 208,000 instead of the 32 million it has today.

There are lovely pictures of Fuling. A couple of thousand years ago it was the capital of the kingdom of Ba. Nowadays, it is the pickle-manufacturing capital of China. Below Fuling is Fengdu, known as the City of Ghosts. The hilltop abodes of the phantoms of Fengdu are high enough to survive, but the rest of the city will be submerged.

There is a fine picture called "The Sentinel of the South," an imposing pagoda that overlooks Wan Hsien (Wanxian), which Mennie claims "guards the city and the river against the malign influence of the 'demons of the South.'" It failed dramatically. Wan Hsien is now an industrial slum. Soon its dark, satanic monosodium glutamate plant and salt mine will sink without trace beneath the waters of progress, but unfortunately 300 historical sites are doomed as well.

We are lucky that such a gifted photographer as Mennie recorded the spectacular beauty of the Three Gorges in all their glory for posterity to admire. Mennie's book was aptly called *The Grandeur of the Gorges*.

*Left*: The city of Wan Hsien is situated between two fine pagodas. The Sentinel of the South, seen here, stands on a hill 800 feet above the river bed. Wan Hsien was a natural fortress surrounded by high hills and fantastic peaks.

*Opposite*: The photographer Donald Mennie described the Witches Gorge as "the longest, most spectacular, and impressive of all the great gorges." The picture was taken in winter. In summer, the turbulent waters rose by a hundred feet.

*Right*: The Wan Hsien bridge. The intrepid traveler Isabella Bird wrote: "I have never seen so beautiful a bridge as the lofty, single stone arch, with a house at the highest part, which spans the river bed, and which seems to spring out of the rock without any visible abutments."

*Below*: The Ching Tan rapids. Captain Cornell Plant, "The Grand Old Man of the Upper Yangtze," lived on the hill in a pavilion attached to the temple of the river god, Wang Yu. It was here that the river pilot wrote his classic *Glimpses of the Yangtze Gorges*.

*Above*: One of the many hill shrines above the misty Vale of Wan. This is a picture of utter serenity. The feeling of peace is an illusion. When Mennie took this photograph in the 1920s, the Vale of Wan was in the very heart of bandit country.

*Right*: The steamer SS *Hung-Fu* making her second attempt to pass the Ye-Tan rapids. It was not until 1898 that Archibald Little's SS *Leechuen* became the first steamer to make the dangerous upriver voyage from Ichang to Chungking. It took Little three weeks to complete the journey.

TURBULENCE AND DECADENCE

# Sir Reginald Johnston: Tutor to the Last Emperor

There was a storm of protest when an anti-missionary book entitled *A Chinese Appeal to Christendom Concerning Christian Missions* was discovered to have been written by Reginald Johnston, a district officer in the leased territory of Weihaiwei, using the Chinese pseudonym Lin Shao-yang. Johnston was a strong supporter of traditional Confucian values and was diametrically opposed to the encroachment of Christianity on the Middle Kingdom.

This may be the reason why, in 1919, he was appointed as English tutor to 14-year-old Pu Yi (Puyi), the last emperor of China. In spite of his Confucian principles, Johnston was at heart a puritanical Scot and he became enormously influential. "Johnston was a major part of my soul," the emperor wrote later.

Apart from flogging the odd eunuch or two for fun, Pu Yi had little to amuse himself in the form of recreation. Johnston introduced him to tennis and cycling in a hopelessly forlorn attempt to turn the boy emperor into some semblance of an English gentleman.

The Manchu courtiers were horrified when Johnston suggested that the emperor, who suffered from severe myopia, should wear glasses. There was no precedent for it; but there was worse to come. Pu Yi decided that he wanted a Western haircut and cut off his own queue with a pair of scissors. When Pu Yi discovered that the eunuchs had been pilfering the palace treasures, he expelled them from the Forbidden City.

Meanwhile, republican China was in the throes of civil war. The Christian General Feng Yu-hsiang, who was rumored to baptize whole regiments of his troops with a fire hose, suddenly seized Peking. The emperor was expelled from the Forbidden City and Johnston lost his job.

Johnston became the last commissioner of Weihaiwei, which true to his Confucian principles, he governed along traditional Ching (Qing) dynasty lines. Two days after the handover of the territory to China in 1930, there were riots. In early 1938, a few weeks after the Rape of Nanking, Japanese imperial forces reoccupied Weihaiwei.

*Left*: An early aerial photograph of the Forbidden City taken before the last emperor was expelled from his palace in 1924. Considering that the picture was shot from an unstable vintage biplane, using slow film, it is a remarkable photograph.

*Opposite left*: Sir Reginald Johnston in Manchu winter costume. Johnston was an eminent Confucian scholar who later governed the British enclave of Weihaiwei with great success, through an eccentric mixture of Chinese jurisprudence and British common law.

*Opposite right*: A formal picture of the Emperor Pu Yi seated on the Dragon Throne. It was taken in 1917, two years before Reginald Johnston was seconded by the British Colonial Office (at the request of the Manchu Court) to be the boy emperor's English tutor.

*Right*: This delightfully casual portrait of Pu Yi's empress, Wan Jung, was taken when the couple were in exile in Tientsin. Tragically, the empress became addicted to opium during this unhappy interlude in the northern treaty port.

*Far right*: Pu Yi in the Tientsin foreign concession where he took refuge after the Christian General Feng Yu-hsiang had expelled him from the Forbidden City. He spent seven years there until, in 1932, the Japanese decided to make him the puppet Emperor of Manchukuo.

TURBULENCE AND DECADENCE 207

# One-Arm Sutton: The Man Who Captured the Great Wall of China

During the warlord period of the 1920s, the arms trade flourished in China. Perhaps the best known "Merchant of Death" was an Old Etonian, One-Arm Sutton. The former British army officer had lost his right arm at Gallipoli. He had invented the Sutton mortar, a lethal little weapon, and he established an arsenal in a mint for General Yang Sen, the warlord of Chungking (Chongqing). He was soon turning out hundreds of mortars. Another warlord, Ma Jui, attempted to capture the mint. Frank Sutton shot him dead in a gunfight reminiscent of the Battle of OK Corral and had to leave Szechwan (Sichuan) in a hurry.

One-arm Sutton later managed the Mukden (Shenyang) arsenal for the great northern warlord, the Old Marshal Chang Tso-lin. He also smuggled arms through Shantung, aided by the infamous Dog-Meat General, Chang Tsung-chang (Zhang Zongchang), who kept a large, exotic, multiracial harem. "He loved a Russian prostitute," wrote Lin Yutang, "and his Russian prostitute loved a poodle, and he made a whole regiment pass in review before the poodle to show that he loved a prostitute that loved a poodle."

The Old Marshal's domain was Manchuria and his objective was to capture Peking, which was held by his enemy, Marshal Wu Pei-fu, but the Great Wall of China stood in the way. Sutton planned to blow a breach in the wall with his mortars, but this proved unnecessary because he found that somebody had left a gate open. The Old Marshal made him a general for this feat of arms. Once again, the Great Wall of China had proved to be "a gigantic useless stone fence."

Sutton became extremely rich after winning the Champions Sweepstake. He owned the most famous racehorse in China, Bengal the Wonder Pony, which he sold to Sir Victor Sassoon after he had decided to leave China before his luck ran out. Sutton went to Canada where he lost half a million pounds sterling during the dark days of the Great Depression.

*Above*: As well as being a swashbuckling adventurer, Frank Sutton was a sportsman extraordinary. At the age of 39, he played rugby for Mukden and scored two tries in an inter-port match against Tientsin. With one arm, he could drive a golf ball 200 yards.

*Opposite below*: The cavalry of the Mongol hordes rode China ponies. These hairy little creatures were used instead of thoroughbred racehorses in the treaty ports. Bengal the Wonder Pony was owned by Sutton. Out of 42 starts, the champion had 41 wins.

*Far left*: The Old Marshal hired Sutton to run his arms arsenal in Mukden. Under Sutton, rifles, machine guns and mortars soon rolled off the primitive assembly line.

*Left*: Marshal Wu Pei-fu was taken completely by surprise when Sutton captured the Great Wall. The road to Peking was now open.

*Below*: The Dog-Meat General, Chang Tsung-chang, a former bandit, was a flamboyant, venal, lecherous and bloodthirsty monster.

TURBULENCE AND DECADENCE

The Great Wall of China, in spite of its size, failed to prevent the wild barbarian tribes from invading China proper and establishing alien Mongol and Manchu dynasties that imposed oppressive foreign rule on the Han Chinese for over a third of the last millennium.

TURBULENCE AND DECADENCE

# Shanghai: The Days of No Tomorrow

China was in turmoil and refugees poured into the treaty ports from all over the country. Merchants were tired of paying tax, sometimes years in advance, every time their home town was captured by a new venal warlord.

Shanghai was the safest haven. Paying protection money to the Green Gang was much cheaper. With them came Tsarist refugees from Soviet Russia and fortune hunters from all over the world.

Shanghai became known as the "City of Sin," for obvious reasons. The nightlife was spectacular, as a local guidebook explains enthusiastically: "High hats and low necks; long tails and short knickers; inebriates and slumming puritans. Wine, women and song. Whoopee! The throb of the jungle tom-tom; the symphony of lust; the music of a hundred orchestras; the shuffling of feet; the rhythm of abandon; the hot smoke of desire—desire under the floodlights; it's all fun."

A Shanghai tailor created the cheongsam and fashionable ladies wore it. So too did the ladies of pleasure who haunted the bars, ballrooms, and that emporium of vice, the Great World Amusement Palace, where the girls on the first floor wore cheongsams slit to their knees; on the second floor the slit reached their thigh and went progressively higher until, on the sixth floor, it hit the armpit. It was a mini-city with restaurants, gambling dens, massage parlors, brothels, ear wax extractors, and midwives.

The Great World was owned by Pockmarked Huang, the head of detectives of the French Sûreté. He was a member of Big-Eared Tu's Green Gang.

The nightclubs, cabarets and ballrooms were legendary: the Canidrome, Venus, Casanova, Metropole, Ciro's, Majestic, and the Caveau Montmartre, which was owned by a Corsican admiral who had been chief-of-staff of warlord Wu Pei-fu.

The contrast between the fun-loving rich and the poor was obscene. Many Chinese refugees made fortunes, but thousands were hopelessly poor and attempted to scrape a living as beggars, hawkers, rickshaw men, coolies, or by working in revolting sweatshops.

**The ballrooms were famed for the beauty of their hostesses. They were run by the great criminal gangs of the Shanghai underworld, the Green Gang, the Blue Gang and the Red Gang, except where the territory was controlled by the Japanese Yakuza.**

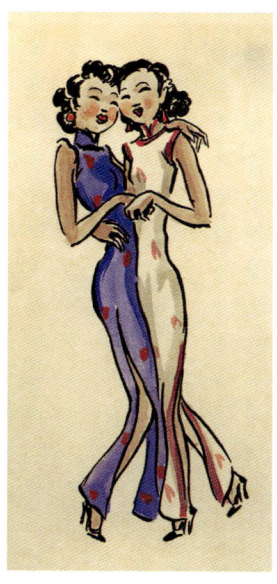  

HAVING A "RIPPING" TIME!

*Left*: The great opulent hotels on the Bund catered for the more sophisticated revellers in search of a "ripping time." There were also hundreds of ballrooms, nightclubs and dens of iniquity. Friedrich Schiff, a talented young Austrian artist, drew these pictures.

*Below*: Gentlemen prefer blondes, especially the rich taipans, who did not always behave like gentlemen. "Night life," advised one Shanghai guidebook, "begins with tea-cocktail hour, tea for propriety, cocktails for pep; it ends at anytime from 2 a.m. until breakfast."

TURBULENCE AND DECADENCE 213

# Cigarette Advertising in the Great Tobacco War

In nineteenth-century America, cigarettes were sold in flimsy paper packets with a card put in as a stiffener for protection. At first these cards were used for advertising, but later picture series appeared which proved to be a great sales gimmick because people collected the sets. These collectors called themselves cartopholists.

Cigarette cards were enormously popular before World War I. This is not surprising as there was no television, and illustrated books and magazines were expensive. It was not until the early 1920s that newspapers printed photographs. Cigarette cards functioned as the poor man's miniature illustrated encyclopedia.

The golden age of Chinese cigarette cards flourished during the Great Tobacco War when the American Tobacco tycoon James "Buck" Duke tried to take over the British tobacco market in China. The Empire fought back and the British formed the Imperial Tobacco Company and tried to put Duke's American Tobacco Company of Shanghai out of business. Both companies produced thousands of cigarette cards to promote the sale of their brands. After years of conflict, eventually peace broke out when the two rival companies formed the British–American Tobacco Company.

The new company continued producing cards that were specially designed for the Chinese market. Chinese tobacco companies soon started printing their own cigarette cards. Cultural themes were popular and there is a fine set of cards with pictures of Peking opera masks. Bathing beauties seem to have been another favorite. The paper shortages in World War II spelt the doom of cigarette cards.

Another attractive product of the Great Tobacco War was the colorful posters produced by the Chinese cigarette companies. They generally featured a glamorous Chinese beauty, fashionably dressed and frequently cuddling a loveable accessory or prop like a pekinese dog, a horse, or even a small child.

Although a packet of the particular brand of the cigarette that the model was advertising appeared discreetly somewhere in the poster, she was never actually pictured smoking or even holding a cigarette.

Original posters are very difficult to find. They are expensive and extremely fragile. Collectors must be very careful. Fakes are run off on photocopiers and can be found in every flea market in China.

**This set of cigarette cards of Chinese beauties was made by Hatamen Cigarettes, a brand manufactured by the British Cigarette Co. Ltd. Sets of cards often featured beautiful women: film stars, bathing beauties, empresses and sometimes even goddesses.**

Mythical figures such as emperors, sages and poets were popular and fairly common subjects. The cards on this page were produced by three different Shanghai tobacco companies. Shanghai was the cigarette manufacturing center of China before World War II.

TURBULENCE AND DECADENCE 215

The originals of these cigarette posters of Chinese beauties were painted in watercolor. It must have been extremely difficult for artists trained in traditional Chinese brush painting to make the successful transition to a Western style of realistic painting.

# Picture Postcards of China

Two Germans, Heinrich von Stephan and Dr Emmanuel Hermann, were credited with inventing postcards, so it is not surprising that it was a Shanghai German company, Kuhn & Komor, which first introduced postcards to China just a couple of years after Sir Robert Hart established the Imperial Post in 1896. Kuhn & Komor's postcards were printed in Germany.

The first picture postcards were grainy black and white and colored by hand. These have a charm of their own. This was years before color photography, and the hand coloring is often quite strange. A red brick building might appear as custard yellow, baby blue or piggy pink, depending on the whim of the colorist. The finest cards were colored in Japan.

The next generation of cards was printed in full color using the halftone process. It took some time for local printers to master this process and many cards manufactured at this time are rather crude with garish colors.

In the 1930s, photographic prints in black and white and sepia became popular. Amateur photographers were able to have their family snaps printed on photographic paper that had a postcard graphic pre-printed on the back. This causes confusion among serious collectors. When is a postcard not a postcard? When it is a commercial postcard perhaps? It is a conundrum.

The best commercial cards are often beautifully printed with incredibly sharp images, but the difference in quality of the printing is so great that it is sometimes quite difficult for purists to tell the difference between a good amateur home-made card and the genuine article.

Postcard collecting was a popular hobby before World War II. Inevitably, these collectors wanted to be called something impressive. They adopted the word deltiologist. It was invented by Randall Rhoades of Ohio and comes from the Greek *deltion*, which means a small picture and can sometimes be found in dictionaries along with other useful words like phillumenist, a moniker loved dearly by enthusiastic collectors of matchboxes.

*Left*: The Shanghai Bund. At the time, the British officers of the Shanghai Police wore Metropolitan Police Force uniforms. In the background can be seen the tower of Sir Robert Hart's Customs House. It was replaced by a new building in 1927.

*Opposite*: Hand-written in French on the front is *Boxer chinois*. Shadow boxing, or *tai chi-chuan*, when translated means "great ultimate fist." It is said to have been developed by the monks of the Shaolin Temple during the Tang dynasty.

This card was printed in Germany and hand-colored in Japan. Before 1905, only the address was allowed to be written on the back of a card. This is why the message is on the front. These are called "single-backed" cards by deltiologists.

No. 688. This picture shows how the Chinese Nurse is carrying a Child by slinging him on her back, leaving her two hands free for Work.

TIBETEAN LAMA.

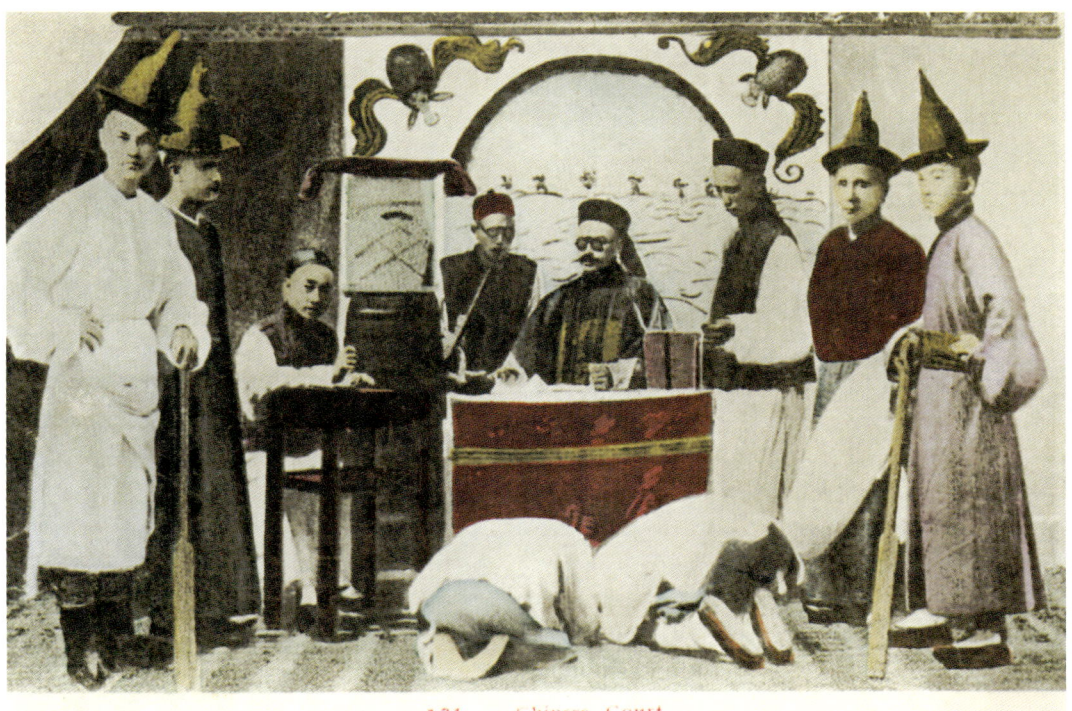

131 Chinese Court

*Above left*: An amah with baby. This traditional way of carrying a baby is still practiced in China today. This postcard was published by M. Sternberg around 1908. Sternberg often used old photographs that were taken in the previous century on his postcards.

*Above right*: A Tibetan Lama with his skull-drum, beads and dorje bell. He is holding his book of Buddhist scriptures. Unlike today, postcards of ethnic minorities were comparatively rare in China during the 1930s when this photograph was taken.

*Left*: Two criminals kowtowing before a magistrate in his *yamen*. This is a mock-up of a Chinese court scene. The costumes of the court officials and the scenery were obviously specially produced for this photograph. The postcard was made for the tourist trade.

TURBULENCE AND DECADENCE 221

# Sun Yat-sen's Bodyguard: General Two-Gun Cohen

Early in life, Morris Cohen established himself as a juvenile delinquent in the East End of London. After he left reform school in 1905, his parents tried to make an honest man out of him. They sent him to a remote ranch in Saskatchewan, Canada, where he made friends with an itinerant cowboy called Bobby Clark who taught him the art of card-sharping and how to cheat at dice.

Consequently, Cohen became a professional gambler. One day he walked into Mah Sam's "chop-suey joint" in Saskatoon to find a lone gunman staging a hold-up. Cohen knocked him out. The lucky punch changed Cohen's life for ever. Mah Sam recruited Cohen to the Tsing Chung-hui Triad Society. This enabled Cohen to auction off the Chinese vote in the Edmonton elections to the highest bidder. When Sun Yat-sen toured Canada, before the Chinese Revolution, Cohen acted as his bodyguard and fell under the great man's spell.

In 1922, the Canadian Northern Construction Company sent Cohen to Shanghai to secure a contract with Sun Yat-sen to build a railway in Southern China. After the deal was signed, Sun Yat-sen hired Cohen as his personal bodyguard.

It was not the easiest job as Sun had little regard for his own personal safety. Fortunately, Cohen found an ally in Sun's wife, Soong Ching-ling (Song Qingling), who was one of the legendary Soong sisters, and foiled a number of assassination attempts. The great Dr Sun Yat-sen died of cancer of the liver in 1925.

Some of Sun's integrity seems to have rubbed off on Cohen. "Honesty," explained Cohen, "can be a kind of racket in itself—and a darned good racket too."

He remained loyal to the Sun family and during World War II flew down from the safety of Chung-king to Hong Kong where he bullied the reluctant Soong Ching-ling into taking the last plane to leave the besieged colony during the Japanese invasion. He was captured by the Japanese, but unlike One-Arm Sutton, he survived the war, married a rich Canadian divorcée and became almost respectable.

Two-Gun Cohen, in the white suit on the right, on bodyguard duty. Standing on the platform from left to right are Liao Chung-Kai, Chiang Kai-shek, Sun Yat-sen and Dr Sun's wife, Soong Ching-ling.

*Far left*: The Flowery Pagoda at Canton is one of the oldest pagodas in southern China. It is said to have been erected in AD 537 during the reign of the Emperor Wu Ti. It was built on an octagonal plan, has nine stories and is 170 feet high.

*Left*: Dr Sun Yat-sen and his wife Soong Ching-ling. She was a daughter of Charlie Soong, the patriarch of the Soong dynasty. Her elder sister Ai-ling married the banker H. H. Kung, and her younger sister Mei-ling became Chiang Kai-shek's wife.

*Below*: The Canton Botanical Gardens were famous for their grotesque shrubs. These plants were attached to wire armatures and trained so as to grow in the shape of dragons, animals, fish and women. Terracotta heads, hands and feet were added later.

TURBULENCE AND DECADENCE

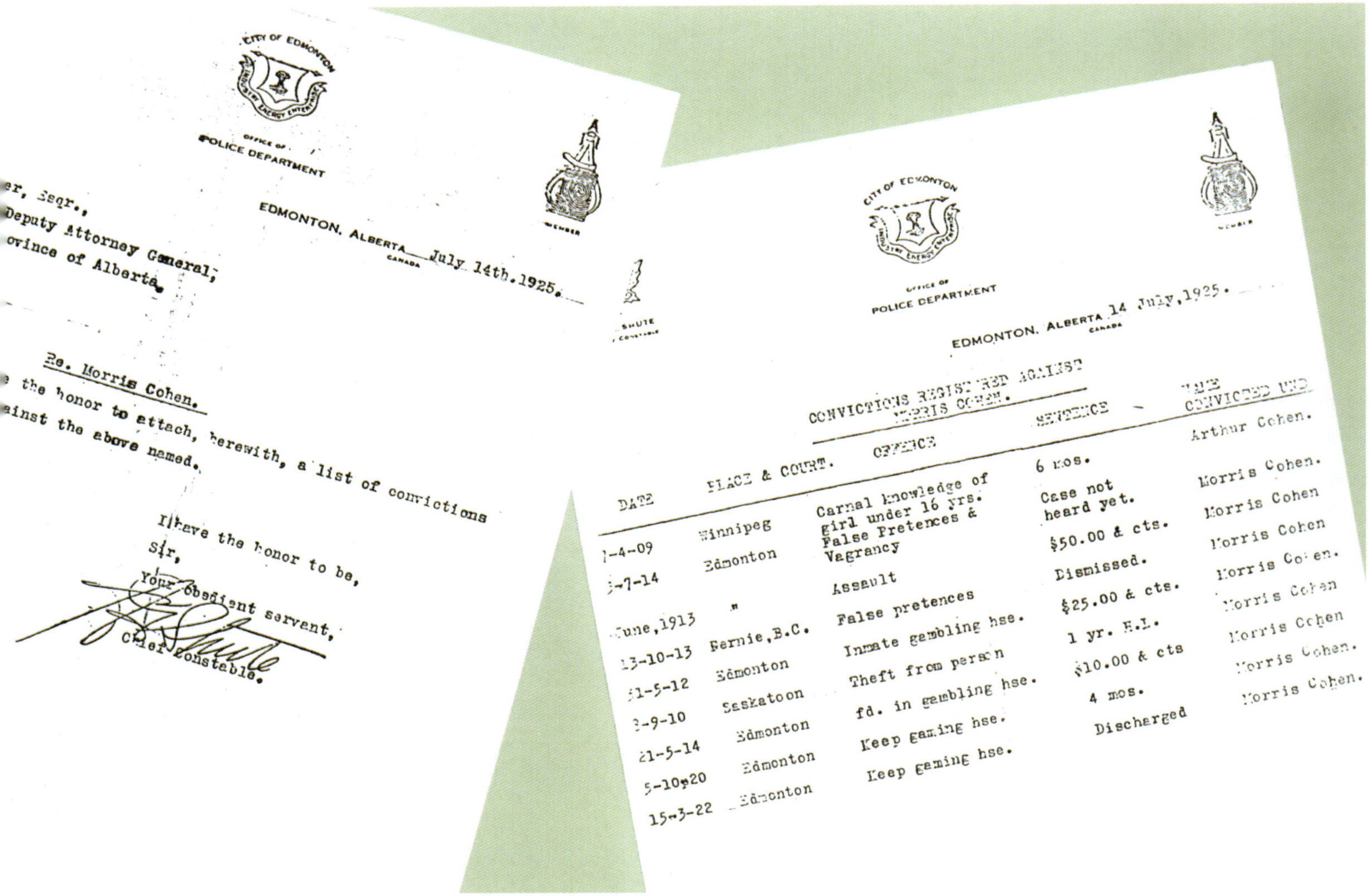

EDMONTON, ALBERTA, July 14th, 1925.

r, Esqr.,
Deputy Attorney General;
ovince of Alberta.

Re. Morris Cohen.

the honor to attach, herewith, a list of convictions
ainst the above named.

I have the honor to be,
Sir,
Your obedient servant,
Chief Constable.

EDMONTON, Alberta, 14 July, 1925.

CONVICTIONS REGISTERED AGAINST MORRIS COHEN.

| DATE | PLACE & COURT | OFFENCE | SENTENCE | NAME CONVICTED UND |
|------|---------------|---------|----------|---------------------|
|  |  |  | 6 mos. | Arthur Cohen. |
| 7-4-09 | Winnipeg | Carnal knowledge of girl under 16 yrs. | Case not heard yet. | Morris Cohen. |
| 3-7-14 | Edmonton | False Pretences & Vagrancy | $50.00 & cts. | Morris Cohen. |
|  |  | Assault | Dismissed. | Morris Cohen. |
| June, 1913 | Fernie, B.C. | False pretences | $25.00 & cts. | Morris Cohen. |
| 13-10-13 | Edmonton | Inmate gambling hse. | 1 yr. H.L. | Morris Cohen. |
| 21-5-12 | Saskatoon | Theft from person fd. in gambling hse. | $10.00 & cts | Morris Cohen. |
| 3-9-10 | Edmonton | Keep gaming hse. | 4 mos. | Morris Cohen. |
| 21-5-14 | Edmonton | Keep gaming hse. | Discharged | Morris Cohen. |
| 5-10-20 | Edmonton |  |  |  |
| 15-3-22 |  |  |  |  |

224 CHINA ILLUSTRATED

*Opposite above*: Cohen's police record. He loved to spin yarns about his criminal career in Edmonton, Canada, where he controlled the Chinese vote through his triad connections. He was introduced to Sun Yat-sen in 1908 by a Canadian politician.

*Opposite below*: During the 1920s, the foreign concession at Shamien became an armed camp. Expatriate residents lived in a state of siege protected by British Indian troops, while opposing warlord and Nationalist factions wreaked havoc.

*Above*: The New Canton Bund was a favorite spot for anti-foreign riots. During one of these incidents, Cohen tipped an unexploded bomb, intended to destroy HMS *Onslaught*, into the Pearl River, thus preventing an international incident.

# The Shanghai Volunteers

The Shanghai Volunteer Corps was raised in 1853 during the Taiping Rebellion to protect the International Settlement. The following year, it fought the Battle of Muddy Flat. In its early years, it was self-supporting: this meant it was in debt. Every volunteer had to pay for his own uniform and rifle. When Harry Parkes became commandant in 1865, it was hopelessly undermanned. He launched a recruiting drive. It failed. The force was disbanded a couple of years later. It was reformed in 1870 after the slaughter of some nuns in Tientsin. This time the Shanghai Municipal Council supplied the arms.

During the Wheelbarrow Riots of 1897, the Volunteers were called out. It had become an international force and the Germans bore the brunt of the riots. Different nations wore different uniforms and an attempt to standardize them failed spectacularly when it came to hats. In 1913, during the Second Revolution, the rebels attacked the Kiangnan (Jiangnan) arsenal. The Volunteers turned out in force and saved the day.

In 1925, the real trouble began. It was the age of the warlords and riots. Shanghai became an armed camp when the nationalist armies advanced on the city. Two companies of White Russians were raised, together with a Filipino platoon and the treaty powers started pouring in thousands of troops. This foreign army was called the Shanghai Defence Force. There were more British soldiers in Shanghai in 1927 than there were in Northern Ireland in the 1980s. They did not stay long and it was left to the Volunteers to guard the International Settlement until Shanghai fell to the Japanese during the Pacific War.

The Shanghai Volunteers was a unique little army. It was an amateur multinational peacekeeping force with an inexhaustible thirst for Ewo beer. Its officers were elected, not appointed. When an officer got fed up being an officer, he would happily revert to the ranks. A couple of years later, he might agree to become an officer again.

**A group of officers of the Shanghai Volunteers.** The variety of national military headgear worn by these amateur soldiers was a unique feature of the regiment, which included English, Scottish, American, Chinese, Japanese, Russian, Portuguese and Jewish companies.

*Above*: The Right Section of the Shanghai Regiment Horse Artillery. The photograph was taken in 1908 during the Ching dynasty. It was commanded by Captain L. E. Canning, who is seen on the left. Canning was later awarded the Order of the British Empire.

*Left*: Soldiers of the Customs Company take time off from the barricades at the corner of Range and Honan Roads during the Second Revolution. The Customs Company was composed of the many different nationalities who worked for the Chinese Customs Service.

*Far left*: The Shanghai Light Horse preparing for an inspection by General Sir George Kirkpatrick. Many of the Volunteers did not own a horse and turned up on parades riding decrepit old hacks with cropped ears, hired from a local livery stable.

*Left*: The Volunteers' artillery stands ready for action during the Second Revolution in 1913, when several provincial warlords attempted to overthrow President Yuan Shih-kai (Yuan Shikai). The Volunteers were mobilized to defend the settlements from the rebels.

*Above*: The Japanese Company at the Markham Road bivouac during the Second Revolution. Seated on the left is the British Commandant of the Volunteers, Lieutenant-Colonel A. A. S. Barnes of the Wiltshire Regiment, a previous commander of the Weihaiwei Regiment.

*Left*: Personnel of the Engineers and Maritime Companies who built this bridge over Soochow Creek in 1918 during the Easter weekend. As well as the infantry and cavalry companies and an armored car company, the Volunteers had a number of miscellaneous units.

TURBULENCE AND DECADENCE

# The Incident on the Blue Express and Other Kidnappings

Thousands of troops deserted the warlord armies to become bandits, and kidnapping became a lucrative occupation. The Chinese suffered the most.

Expatriates were not immune. In 1923, bandits attacked the Blue Express in Shantung and kidnapped 200 foreigners. For ten days they were marched barefoot in their nightclothes to the bandits' stronghold in the mountains. Among those kidnapped was Lucy Aldrich, the sister-in-law of John D. Rockefeller, Jr. Her French maid hid Lucy's fabulous jewels in a rice field. Another prisoner, John B. Powell, an American journalist, managed to smuggle out a report to the *China Weekly Review*. The Red Cross representative, Carl Crow, a smooth-talking advertising man, secured their release and Lucy Aldrich's jewels were later recovered.

In Manchuria, bandits kidnapped Harvey Howard, an American doctor. The local warlord, Old Marshal Chang Tso-lin, was furious and sent a small army to the rescue. For ten weeks Chang's troops chased the bandits through three provinces. Howard saved his life by making friends with his kidnappers. The doctor tended their sick and wounded. They called him the "Hairy One." Chu Mao-ju, another prisoner, was not so lucky—he was murdered. The Old Marshal was an ex-bandit himself and it would have been a loss of face for him to pay a ransom.

His troops rescued the Hairy One in a dramatic attack on the kidnappers' camp. Because no bandits were killed, Howard reckoned that the Old Marshal had secretly paid the ransom. His suspicion was confirmed when a few years later one of his bloodthirsty bandit "friends" wrote to him asking him for a job.

After Generalissimo Chiang Kai-shek captured Shanghai, he no longer thought it necessary to pay protection money to Big-Eared Tu, the godfather of the Green Gang. Chiang foolishly considered himself more powerful than the Shanghai underworld. It was a serious mistake. Tu's chauffeur enticed Chiang's bride Soong Mei-ling (Song Meiling) into a Rolls Royce by explaining that it had been sent by "her sister." The Soong family paid up and the kidnapping was kept a secret for years.

*Far left*: Dr Harvey Howard before his kidnapping. The bandits' intended victim was a rich American farmer, William Palmer, who owned a model ranch. Unfortunately, the bandits shot Palmer and kidnapped Howard, a Professor of Ophthalmology, by mistake.

*Left*: Dr Howard after he had been rescued. The bandits called him the "Hairy One." He lost eight inches around his waist during his nine weeks of captivity. He was convinced that it was his skills as a doctor that probably saved him from being murdered.

*Far left*: Big-Eared Tu, the godfather of the Green Gang. His gangsters, supported by a number of Chiang Kai-shek's soldiers in civilian clothes, massacred thousands of Communists and their left-wing allies during a surprise attack on them, known as the White Terror.

*Left*: The young Chou En-lai was one of the Communist leaders during Chiang Kai-shek's coup. Chou was lucky to escape being killed by the Green Gang during the fight for the General Union Building.

*Below*: Regular troops of the US Army parade on the racecourse during the 1927 crisis. They were part of the Shanghai Defence Force formed by Treaty Powers composed of eight different nations to defend their interests in Shanghai's International Settlement.

TURBULENCE AND DECADENCE 235

*Above*: The International Settlement showing Garden Bridge in the foreground. In 1927, when Chiang Kai-shek's armies of the Northern Expedition advanced on Shanghai, the city was panic-stricken. At the time, the Shanghailanders were under the illusion that Chiang Kai-shek was a Communist.

*Left*: HMS *Vindictive* was one of the 42 foreign warships anchored in Shanghai after the left-wing faction of the Northern Expedition of the advancing Nationalist forces had captured Hankow and forced the British to return their foreign concession to China.

*Opposite*: The American Marines manning this barricade were a unit of the Shanghai Defence Force which was sent by the Treaty Powers to protect the concessions from Chiang Kai-shek's advancing armies. In May 1927, there were 40,000 foreign troops in Shanghai.

TURBULENCE AND DECADENCE

# Chapter 5

# NATIONALISTIC CHINA AT PEACE AND WAR
## (1928–1941)

In the year after the White Terror, when Chiang Kai-shek had almost annihilated the Chinese Communist Party, he consolidated his power base in central and southern China. The Christian general had allied himself with Chiang and became his minister of war. Peking (Beijing) was in the control of Old Marshal Chang Tso-lin (Zhang Zuolin), but his position was shaky so he decided to withdraw to his stronghold in Manchuria.

In June 1928, the Old Marshal left Peking for Manchuria by train. It was blown up outside Mukden by the Japanese, killing the marshal. Five days later, the Model Governor, Yen Hsi-shan (Yan Xishan), who was also allied to the Kuomintang (Guomindang), marched into Peking unopposed.

In Manchuria, the Old Marshal's son, the Young Marshal Chang Hsueh-liang (Zhang Xueliang), seized power and pledged his allegiance to the Nationalist government. The Manchurian generals and the Japanese had not considered him as a threat because he had the reputation of being an opium addict and was rather over fond of actresses. The Young Marshal may have had his faults, but he was a dedicated patriot, unlike many of the other warlords. This did not suit the Japanese.

The Japanese, with their forces in Korea, Tsingtao (Qingdao) and a naval base at Port Arthur (Lushun), were well placed to invade Manchuria. Their chance came in 1931 when a bomb exploded on the Japanese South Manchurian Railway outside Mukden. The Japanese used this as an excuse for their army to take over the city. Their timing was perfect. The Young Marshal was in Peking at the time, attempting to cure his opium addiction.

Dozens of foreign correspondents arrived in the city. Among them was John B. Powell (of the Blue Express kidnapping) who was now representing the *Manchester Guardian* and *Chicago Tribune*. He was not the only journalist to smell a rat. Powell wrote, "I found a large collection of pictures showing Japanese in plain clothes bearing rifles and wearing arm bands. Foreign businessmen testified that Mukden had been overrun several days prior to September 18, 1931, by large groups of Japanese 'tourists' wearing civilian clothes." He concluded that "It is well to keep this date in mind, as it was the real beginning of World War II."

To give their invasion some credibility, the Japanese set up the puppet state of Manchukuo and appointed the deposed Ching (Qing) emperor Pu Yi (Puyi) as its chief executive and later as its emperor. Pu Yi had been living under the protection of the Japanese in Tientsin (Tianjin) after the Christian general had thrown him out of the Forbidden City. Here he came under the influence of the Japanese agent Yoshiko Kawashima, who was actually a Manchu princess and a distant relative of the emperor. She was the daughter of Prince Su who had been involved in a failed conspiracy in Mongolia to restore the Ching. He had sent her to be educated in Japan. Myth, propaganda and history tend to get muddled about Yoshiko.

It is probably fiction that she had a lesbian affair with Pu Yi's empress, Wan Jung (Wanrong). In real life, her principal lover was Ryukichi Tanaka, a high-ranking Japanese intelligence officer. Yoshiko loved to dress in male clothes and the stories about her are often incredible, but could easily be true, because the woman was capable

*Left*: Pu Yi in military uniform. He was made the puppet Emperor of Manchukuo by the Japanese. After World War II, he was imprisoned as a war criminal, but was pardoned by Mao Tse-tung in 1959 and spent his old age working as a gardener.

*Below*: The Empress Wan Jung refused to accompany her husband to Port Arthur when he sought Japanese protection. She was persuaded to change her mind by Pu Yi's cousin, Yoshiko Kawashima, a Manchu princess who was a notorious Japanese agent.

*Above*: Chinese soldiers on the Marco Polo Bridge. In 1937, the Japanese bombarded Wanping because the Chinese refused to let them search the town for a missing Japanese soldier. The Marco Polo Bridge Incident officially marks the beginning of the anti-Japanese War.

*Right*: Generalissimo Chiang Kai-shek established a Nationalist government in Nanking after the success of the Northern Expedition in 1927. Ten years later, following the Rape of Nanking, Chiang moved his government to Chungking (Chongqing).

*Far right*: The Young Marshal kidnapped Chiang Kai-shek and forced him to join a United Front with the Communists against the Japanese. The Generalissimo had flown to Sian in order to try to persuade the Young Marshal to fight against the Communists.

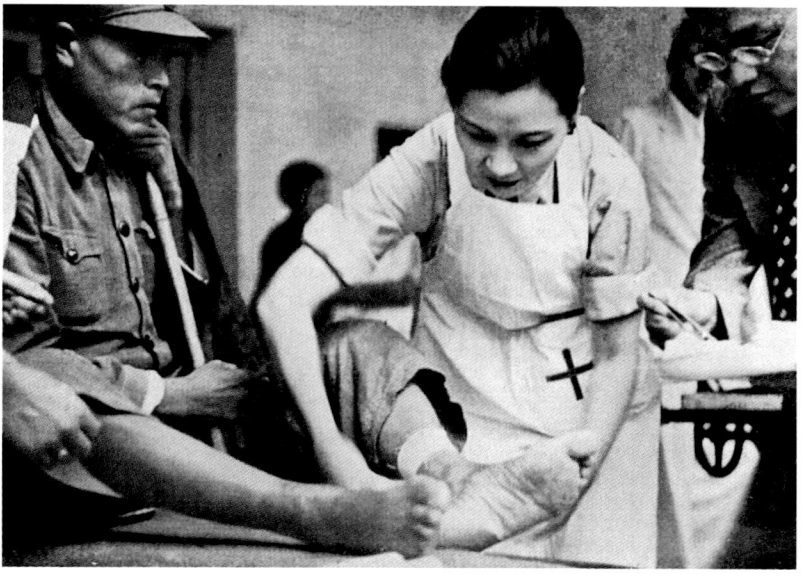

Madame Chiang Kai-shek demonstrates her skills at First Aid by bandaging the foot of a wounded soldier when visiting the 64th Base Hospital at Hankow in 1938. During her visit, she delivered a consignment of medical supplies donated by the people of America.

of anything. She has been accused of taking part in Japanese air raids in 1932, when Japan bombed and strafed the Chinese areas of Shanghai after an anti-Japanese riot.

While the Young Marshal's forces were waging a guerrilla war in Manchuria, Chiang Kai-shek turned his attention to the Communists who had regrouped and established the Kiangsi (Jiangxi) Soviet. Together Mao Tse-tung (Mao Zedong) and Chu Teh (Zhu De) had formed the Red Army. After a series of anti-Communist Extermination Campaigns, the Red Army decided to move to a safer base in northern China closer to the border with Soviet Russia. The Long March began in October 1934.

It took over a year and what was left of the army arrived in Shensi (Shaanxi) and established a base at Yenan. From the original 86,000 who had began, only 8,000 survived the 4,000-mile march.

Chiang Kai-shek, who was alarmed at the revival of the Red Army as a fighting force, ordered the Young Marshal Chang Hsueh-liang to exterminate the survivors. The Young Marshal, driven out of Manchuria by the Japanese who had murdered his father, felt very strongly that fighting the invaders was more important than killing fellow Chinese and declined to obey the order. Chiang Kai-shek flew to Sian (Xian) in an attempt to persuade him to change his mind. The Young Marshal's reaction was to attack the house where Chiang was staying. His soldiers chased the Generalissimo up a hill in his nightshirt and kidnapped him. With Chiang in his power, the Young Marshal opened negotiations with the Communists.

Mao Tse-tung sent Chou En-lai (Zhou Enlai) to Sian for discussions and Chiang Kai-shek was forced to form the Second United Front allied with the Communists in the war against Japan. After the Sian Incident, the Young Marshal accompanied Chiang Kai-shek back to Nanking (Nanjing) and he was placed under house arrest. He was to remain in captivity for decades. When he died in Hawaii in 2001 at the age of 100, he was still known as the Young Marshal.

In 1937, after the Marco Polo Bridge Incident, the Japanese launched another offensive in central China and captured Shanghai and Nanking. The year 1937 is the generally accepted date for the beginning of the Sino-Japanese War, although Chiang Kai-shek, who had moved his government to Chungking, did not actually declare war on Japan until after Pearl Harbor. As the two countries were not technically at war in the 1930s, battles and massacres tended to be described as "incidents" by the propaganda machines of both sides. This reflected the Generalissimo's strategy of appeasement and suited the Japanese "bandit pacification campaigns" admirably.

The early 1930s were known as the heyday of Nationalist rule. Chiang Kai-shek had married Soong Mei-ling (Song Meiling), the younger sister of Soong Ai-ling (Song Ailing) and Soong Ching-ling (Song Qingling). It was said of the Soong Sisters: "One loved money, one loved power and one loved China." Ai-ling's husband was the fabulously rich industrialist H. H. Kung (who later became Chiang's finance minister) and Ching-ling was the widow of Sun Yat-sen. The Soong dynasty, as it was known, was founded by an American-educated Bible publisher who called himself Charlie Soong and had been a prominent supporter of Sun Yat-sen. Charlie also had three sons,

*Above*: Mao Tse-tung on the march in 1947. This picture was taken a decade after the famous Long March, when the Chinese Communist armies retreating from Nationalist forces walked thousands of miles to Yenan, where they successfully regrouped.

*Right*: Boy Scouts on a parade in Nanking in 1936. They were the vanguard of the New Life Movement. During the fighting, Boy Scouts were frequently attached to Red Cross trucks and sent to the front, where they helped collect the wounded on the battlefield.

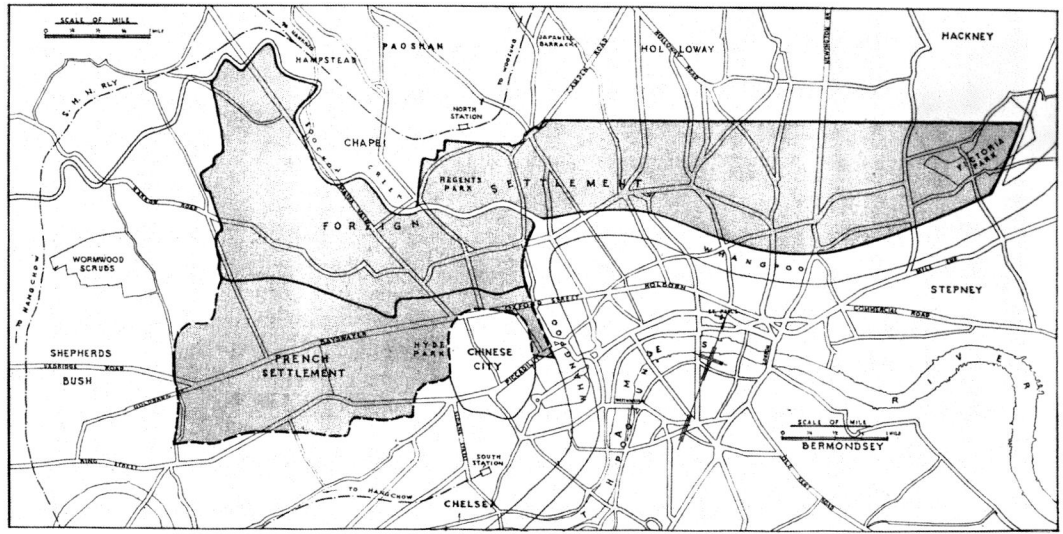

This map of Shanghai, superimposed on a map of London, was published by the *North-China Daily News & Herald* in 1932. The Foreign Settlement is shaded. Shanghai's old walled city was almost one-third the area of London's Hyde Park.

THE FOREIGN SETTLEMENTS OF SHANGHAI COMPARED WITH LONDON

The above Sketch Map has been prepared to give an idea of the extent of Shanghai as compared with London. The Foreign Settlements (shaded) and the surrounding thickly populated districts have been superimposed on a Map of London drawn to scale. It will be seen that our Western Boundary is nearly level with Hammersmith Bridge, while our Eastern Boundary covers Victoria Park. The Chinese City has room to spare in Hyde Park.

including T. V. Soong, who was at different times Chiang's prime minister, foreign minister, finance minister and just about everything else. T. V.'s brothers, T. L. Soong and T. A. Soong were both bankers and financiers. The Soongs and their relations were the most powerful family in Nationalist China. Chiang Kai-shek married Mei-ling only after his unwelcome advances were turned down by Sun Yat-sen's widow Ching-ling who loathed the Generalissimo for betraying her dead husband's principles.

To counterbalance the Communists' propaganda machine, Madame Chiang Kai-shek formed the New Life Movement. Foreigners in the treaty port were confused about its aims. Initially, it was run by the police and the boy scouts. Christopher Isherwood, who visited China in 1938 with the poet W. H. Auden to research a book, described it as "a curious moral crusade." The left-wing opinion was that the Movement was something similar to Hitler Youth, whereas others welcomed it and claimed that it promoted "the traditional Chinese values of propriety, righteousness, integrity and a sense of shame."

When Isherwood and Auden asked the Mayor of Canton to explain, he replied enigmatically, "New Life is not *under* and not *over* human nature." They later asked Madame Chiang the same question. Isherwood wrote, "Madame, we were bound to admit, made all this sound eminently practical and sensible: 'To Europeans, our virtue of Outward Propriety may seem rather silly. But China has forgotten these things, and so they are important.'

The anti-rubbish campaign was not terribly practical in the middle of war when millions of people in China were starving and its cities and villages were in ruins.

Isherwood wrote, "On the way back to Hankow we discussed the Movement and the Chiang régime. Could China ever be cleaned up? Auden himself, a veteran enemy of compulsory hygiene, was sceptical."

In spite of the war, the treaty ports were havens of trade and flourished up until the Rape of Nanking by the Japanese in 1937. The expatriate population had 200 years' experience of living in a fool's paradise. They had weathered the Opium War, the Boxer Rebellion, the Chinese Revolution and the warlord period, so the optimists believed that this was just another phase in China's blood-soaked history.

Isolated in their own unreal world of tea on the lawn, tiffin, a day at the races and dinner parties, the more respectable citizens thought that "the troubles" would pass, as they had always done. Others, like the doctors, missionaries, journalists and social workers thought otherwise, if they had time to think, as they worked themselves to death helping the millions of refugees and wounded.

The decadent did not seem to care much anyway and drank their way through the fleshpots of the great cities. Their hedonistic philosophy was the familiar "eat, drink and be merry, for tomorrow we die."

When World War II broke out in Europe, even the most befuddled drunk realized that this was the beginning of the end. After the Japanese bombed Pearl Harbor on 7 December 1941, the President of the United States, Franklin Delano Roosevelt, denounced the pre-emptive strike on the American Fleet as "the day of infamy." The Chinese had suffered too many "days of infamy" over the previous century to be particularly surprised by the attack.

# The Pursuit of Wealth

There are few better examples of having all your eggs in one basket than Shanghai before World War II, where the wealth of China was hoarded in the vaults of the foreign banks. Trade figures show that in 1929 China was exporting US $1,070 million worth of goods. Imports were up to $2,002 million in 1931. Shanghai controlled over 50 percent of China's foreign trade and just under 40 percent of domestic trade.

There were thousands of small factories in the Chinese municipality where refugees provided cheap labor. The great Shanghainese entrepreneur race tended to live in the International Settlement close to their money. The Nanking Road was the Bond Street and Fifth Avenue of Shanghai rolled into one. It was famous for its fabulous department stores: Wing On, Sincere and Sun Sun.

Peking (Beijing) was the center of the antique and curio trade and was well supplied with loot by the warlord armies. There was the famous Street of Silks for collectors of Mandarin robes, and others specializing in jade and porcelain. The Asian system of streets of shops selling the same product was particularly irritating when shopping on a more humble scale. The Street of Nails was invariably miles away from the Street of Hammers.

Small traders, hawkers and food stalls were to be found even in the smartest thoroughfares. They were protected by the triads in league with the local King of Beggars, who would send some wretched cripple covered in sores to sit outside a shop, where he molested prospective customers until the shopkeeper paid him to go away. Rampart corruption and squeeze were endemic in every stratum of society throughout China.

In the larger treaty ports like Shanghai, the Settlement Police were stricter, but wary, because it was easy enough to start an anti-foreign riot in Nationalist China where conspicuous opulence, wealth and hopeless poverty stalked the streets hand in hand.

Shanghai's Foochow Road ran from the Hongkong and Shanghai Bank building on the Bund to the Thibet Road near the racecourse. As well as being a shoppers' paradise, many of the great international companies had offices there.

*Left*: The Bund at Shanghai started life as a coolie towpath on the banks of the Whangpoo River. The British and French developed it into a wide promenade between the city and the river, with lovely gardens and busy passenger jetties.

*Above*: The ceiling of the dome of the Hongkong and Shanghai Bank building. The mosaic panels represent the great banking centers of the East and the West. An inscription which circles the dome reads "Within the Four Seas All Men are Brothers."

*Left*: The Nanking Road was the main artery of Shanghai. It was dominated by the exotic spires of the great Chinese department stores Sun Sun, Wing On and Sincere. This fabulous shopping street was also known as the "Great White Way."

The Shanghai Bund looking north. Bunds were the original commercial centers of most treaty ports. *Bund* is the Hindi word for an artificial waterside embankment or quay. In Hong Kong and Macau, the Portuguese word *praya* was used.

*Above*: The scrollmakers street in the old Chinese Walled City of Shanghai. To the north were the French Concession and the International Settlement. Surrounding the old city and the foreign concessions was a vast new Chinese municipality with a population of millions.

*Left*: The massive Hongkong and Shanghai Bank building on the Bund was opened for business in 1923. Although it was only a branch office, no expense was spared in creating this opulent and magnificent monument to Mammon.

NATIONALISTIC CHINA AT PEACE AND WAR 247

*Above left*: It is always easier to produce effective advertising for the luxury market than to achieve success at grassroots level. Carl Crow's classic *400 Million Customers* is an hilarious account of his struggle to introduce Western advertising to China's masses.

*Above right*: Magazine advertisements were often extremely sophisticated and followed the style and fashions of Europe and America. This beautiful Art Deco travel advertisement would not have looked out of place in *Vogue*, *Harper's Bazar*, *Vanity Fair* or *La Vie Parisienne*.

*Left*: An image similar to Andy Warhol's "Campbell's Soup." He was only six years old when this striking advertisement appeared in *The China Journal*. "They say that time changes things," wrote Warhol, "but you actually have to change them yourself."

*Opposite*: Crow claimed that his advertising agency was responsible for placing the first lipstick advertisement in a Chinese newspaper in the early 1920s.

# The Westernized Chinese

In the 1930s, it was considered extremely modern by many of the Chinese bourgeoisie to become thoroughly Westernized. Women had been considered little more than chattels in imperial China, but with the country becoming a republic the emancipation of women suddenly became a welcome reality. Militant middle-class housewives formed the vanguard of change.

Madame Yang and her family lived on the campus of Yenching University in Peking (Beijing) where most of the other staff were Americans. Madame Yang was a Western lifestyle convert. She smoked Pall Mall cigarettes, drank martinis, breastfed her babies and her house furnishings were *Homes and Gardens* chic.

Katherine Wei, in her delightful book, *Second Daughter*, described her mother's parties where the children, dressed in tiny tartan skirts and Christopher Robin shoes, performed their party piece: "Alice would walk directly to the spinet and rap out 'Jeepers, Creepers,' to which I would do a frantic Charleston, incorporating every last one of the knee-gripping, arm-flailing, and heel-slapping bits Mother had studied in some 1920s film."

The Westernized Chinese were frequently ridiculed by their fellow countrymen. Lao She, the author of *Rickshaw Boy*, wrote a satire on a "West is best" Chinese who boasted of a doctorate from Harvard. "In his eyes," wrote Lao, "all Chinese are like the Chinese portrayed in American movies." His maxim was "You must do things with the American spirit, you must do things the American way!"

The doctor was obsessed with women and Hollywood films. When asked about Peking opera, he replied with a sneer, "From what I hear from my foreign friends, the Chinese theater is barbarous!"

In spite of talking about little other than movies and women, the doctor never took out girls, because dating the American way was too expensive. So his friends were surprised when he suddenly became engaged to a Shanghainese girl. They were invited to the marriage ceremony which took place, predictably, in an American church. The beautifully engraved wedding invitation, also predictably, was written in English.

A still from the Chinese film *Angel*, made in 1939. More than 90 percent of the films shown in China's 250 cinemas at the time were American, in spite of the top three Chinese studios producing on average about six films a month.

*Left*: A clash of cultures was a common feature in the cosmopolitan treaty ports, where people of all nations, rich and poor, lived, played and worked in close proximity to each other. Everyday scenes like this were a gift to a talented cartoonist.

*Below left*: The traditional Chinese wedding was a complicated ceremony that went on for three days. Humiliating rituals, where the bride had to grovel to her mother-in-law, could be avoided by having a modern Western-style wedding at a fraction of the cost.

*Below center*: A portrait of Sun Yat-sen and his wife Soong Ching-ling taken in 1919. Dr Sun, unlike his wife, preferred to wear formal Western clothes with the notable exception of any form of military uniform, which the old revolutionary detested.

*Below right*: The father and children of a Westernized family would generally wear foreign clothes, while the wife would wear a *cheong sam*. The family tended to eat Chinese food, "because the Westerners all say that Chinese cooking is the best and most wholesome."

*Right*: Foreign female fashions were all the rage in the treaty ports. The "West is Best" phenomenon was not confined to the modern, wealthy and militant middle class. Film stars, sing-song girls and even the humble amah were not immune.

*Below left*: Miss Hsui Tsai-ying was a famous Tientsin ballet artist and singer. She is seen here elegantly posed against an Art Deco backdrop. The treaty port of Tientsin was the fashion center of northern China and was second only to Shanghai in the country.

*Below center*: A Nanking sing-song girl called "Miss Snow and Guitar" in Manchu costume.

*Below right*: Miss Snow relaxing in Western dress. In 1936, most of the 300 registered sing-song girls in Nanking underwent government training as military nurses.

A publicity picture of Wong Jen-mei, a famous Chinese movie star. Miss Wong wears a Western dress, sports a Western hairstyle and wears Western shoes. She is sitting on a Western claw-footed upholstered stool. Even the parquet floor is typically Western.

An illustration by Sam for Lu Hsun's short story, *A Happy Family*. The story is a satire about a highly intellectual Chinese couple who were both educated in America and the problems that they faced readjusting to life in China.

NATIONALISTIC CHINA AT PEACE AND WAR

# The Great Espionage Epidemic

Shanghai in the 1930s was a bit like Casablanca in the 1940s: it was a nest of spies. Every powerful nation or political movement had an active network of secret agents and informers in China's wealthiest city.

The Black Dragon Society was the espionage arm of the Japanese army. It employed thousands of spies and *agents provocateurs*. Its members called themselves *ronin* after the masterless legendary samurai swordsmen. They were basically terrorists and created incidents that incited the Chinese to riot. This provided an excuse for the Japanese to send in the marines.

The Russians' espionage network had been destroyed during the White Terror. Their new spymaster in China was Richard Sorge. Agnes Smedley, an American journalist, introduced him to Ozaki Hotsumi, later the key figure in his Japanese network. Sorge did not employ Russians, who were suspect, or women if he could help it. He tolerated Smedley because, as he said, "she looks like a man."

Sorge was an Austrian who had joined the Nazi party in order to spy on the Germans, but became a double agent. The Germans also used Trebitsch Lincoln, who was possibly a quadruple agent. Lincoln was a Hungarian Jew who claimed to admire Hitler. Although the British Special Branch of the Shanghai Police knew about Smedley's and Lincoln's activities, they chose to watch them rather than arrest them. The Special Branch had a very long list of spies. It included drug dealers, actors, abortionists, prostitutes and journalists. Sorge, although a journalist, was not on their list.

The British secret agents were much more respectable. Their chief was John Keswick, a taipan of Jardine Matheson, whose brother, William Keswick, also a spy, was chairman of the Shanghai Municipal Council.

Every warlord and Chinese political party had secret agents. The Kuomintang's intelligence chiefs were Tai Li (Dai Li), the "Himmler of China," and Two-Gun Cohen. They also used the Green Gang. The Communists' network was run by the gruesome Kang Sheng. This monster is now vilified in China for his part in the Great Leap Forward and the Cultural Revolution.

*Left*: Trebitsch Lincoln, aka Abbot Chao Kung, was probably the most unsuccessful spy in China because every intelligence agency was familiar with his notorious past.

*Center*: During World War II, American journalist Agnes Smedley became an adviser to General "Vinegar Joe" Stilwell. She persuaded him to supply arms to the Red Army.

*Right*: Richard Sorge was Russia's spymaster in China and Japan. Stalin did not believe Sorge's intelligence. When Sorge predicted the Japanese attack on Pearl Harbor, Stalin did not tell his ally Britain.

*Left*: The Shanghai Municipal Police in the International Settlement were tightly controlled by the British although the force included Sikh, Chinese, White Russian and Japanese officers. The Special Branch was known to work closely with British Military Intelligence.

*Below*: The French Concession in Shanghai was a safe haven for spies, revolutionaries, conmen and gangsters like Big-Eared Tu. This was because the French Sûreté was corrupt and seldom co-operated with the Special Branch of the International Settlement.

# Photographers of the 1920s and 1930s

Perhaps the most admired photographer of the time was Donald Mennie. He was a perfectionist. He took his pictures in soft focus, which was fashionable in the age of Post-Impressionist art. This was an advantage because his books were printed in photogravure where the image is etched on a copper plate. He enhanced the images by burnishing the copper plates before printing. Nowadays we use a computer.

The plates were printed in "eleven soft colours." Most books today use the four-color process. Multiple colors are used only in very expensive gallery prints.

Fortunately, Mennie was a very rich man. He was the taipan of A. S. Watson & Co., the leading chain of dispensaries in China. He has often been classified as an "amateur," but there is nothing amateur about his work.

Another photographer who used this technique was Heinz von Perckhammer. He specialized in nudes of pubescent Chinese girls. He complained that he had difficulty in finding models. He also had problems with studio lighting, but seems to have been unaware of this. His book, *Edle Nacktheit in China*, is much prized by collectors for reasons other than art. Fortunately, the photographs he took in natural light were brilliant.

Many of the best photographers seemed to have been German or war photographers. The most memorable image of the period was actually taken by a Chinese news cameraman called "Newsreel" Wong. He even used this name on his passport. He worked as cameraman for Fox Movietone News, but always carried a still camera. He took the famous picture of a baby crying among the ruins of a railway station at Shanghai. He loved to tell his fellow newsmen how he shot this photograph.

There were always beggars at railway stations in China. "Newsreel" borrowed the little mite from his mother, rubbed some charcoal over his face and posed him among the ruins. Unfortunately, the baby gurgled and giggled happily and refused to cry. "So I slapped him!" said "Newsreel", "And got the picture."

*Left*: On the Grand Canal. Rather than enhancing his work in the darkroom, Donald Mennie preferred to enrich his images by working on copper plates during the photogravure process, instead of printing directly on photographic paper like other photographers.

*Opposite*: The Red Boats. They belonged to a lifeboat service that operated on the turbulent waters of the Yangtze within the Three Gorges. As well as sails, they had a crew of six oarsmen. The picture is a fine example of Mennie's use of "eleven soft colours."

Nude with flower by Heinz von Perckhammer. This famous photograph comes from his book *Edle Nacktheit in China*. He never really mastered studio lighting, but fortunately his pictures of people that were taken in natural light were superb.

*Above right*: The mother-in-law, by Ellen Thorbecke. Filial piety obliged her sons to hand over their wages to their mother, who was a widow. Their wives did all the household chores. This ancient matriarch spent her old age in complete control of her family's lives.

*Right*: A baby crying among the bomb wreckage of Shanghai South Station. This famous picture was taken during the Japanese attack on Shanghai in 1932. News pictures in the 1930s tended to be stark "soot-and-whitewash." Photograph by "Newsreel" Wong.

# The Japanese Attack on Shanghai (1932)

Marshal Blücher once said of London, "What a place to plunder!" The Japanese had similar feelings about Shanghai a century later. They cynically played the old Christian imperialist trick of using missionaries to enrage the local populace and then sending in gunboats and land troops to restore order.

Their *agents provocateurs* were five maniacal Japanese monks who were members of the Black Dragon Society. They gave an impromptu concert in a Chinese factory where they sang Japanese songs which praised their countrymen's glorious victory over the Chinese in Manchuria. This belligerent performance provoked a riot and one monk was killed by the mob.

The incident provided the Japanese with the excuse to land 1,200 marines. They ordered the Chinese Nineteenth Route Army, which was stationed in the city, to withdraw. To their surprise, the army commander, General Tsai Ting-kai (Cai Tingkai), would not be bullied and refused to budge. The Japanese attacked and for thirty-four days the Chinese resisted valiantly. Only the arrival of 55,000 reinforcements from Japan compelled General Tsai to retreat. Eighteen thousand civilians were killed or missing and 240,000 people lost their homes.

The British, Americans and French poured in troops as fast as they could in support of the Shanghai Volunteers who were guarding the Foreign Settlement. They were joined by a small force of Hong Kong Volunteers, who had hurriedly been recruited in the colony. Among these recruits were two conmen named Errol Flynn and Hermann Erben, who had joined up because they were broke. The two villains arrived in Shanghai after the shooting had stopped. They spent a few days digging trenches in the snow before they deserted. Errol Flynn became a film star and Erben eventually joined the Gestapo. Erben was a naturalized American citizen and by joining a foreign army (the Hong Kong Volunteers) his citizenship had been automatically revoked. This saved him from being jailed for treason after the war.

Soldiers of the Nineteenth Route Army at the barricades. The Japanese had expected a walkover. General Tsai Ting-kai and his men had other ideas. However, they received no support from Chiang Kai-shek who stuck to his policy of appeasement.

*Left*: An Errol Flynn look-alike on guard outside Elgin Road School. Flynn and his friend Hermann Erben joined the Hong Kong Volunteers during the crisis and were sent to Shanghai. They arrived after the fighting was over and deserted three weeks later.

*Below*: Japanese troops in action. The original Japanese attacking force was 1,200 marines. A month later, it had been increased by 55,000 reinforcements that included tanks and field artillery. Copies of this famous picture were sold everywhere in Shanghai after the conflict.

NATIONALISTIC CHINA AT PEACE AND WAR

*Opposite*: A Manchu lady takes a rickshaw ride on a foggy day in Peking. Even in monochrome, the influence of Post-Impressionist painting on Donald Mennie's work is evident. Soft focus photography was very fashionable in the 1920s and 1930s.

*Above*: Mennie's Lamplight Gorge. Achieving perfect balance is a rare skill in photography. Like perfect pitch in music, it is a gift from the gods. It cannot be learnt. Artists, architects and designers call it "the eye." You either have it or you don't.

*Right*: Sometimes thousands of mourners took part in the funeral processions of the rich and famous. Mourning trumpeters accompanied the coffin. The wealthier the deceased, the more extravagant the ceremony. Photograph by the German photographer and journalist Ellen Thorbecke.

NATIONALISTIC CHINA AT PEACE AND WAR   263

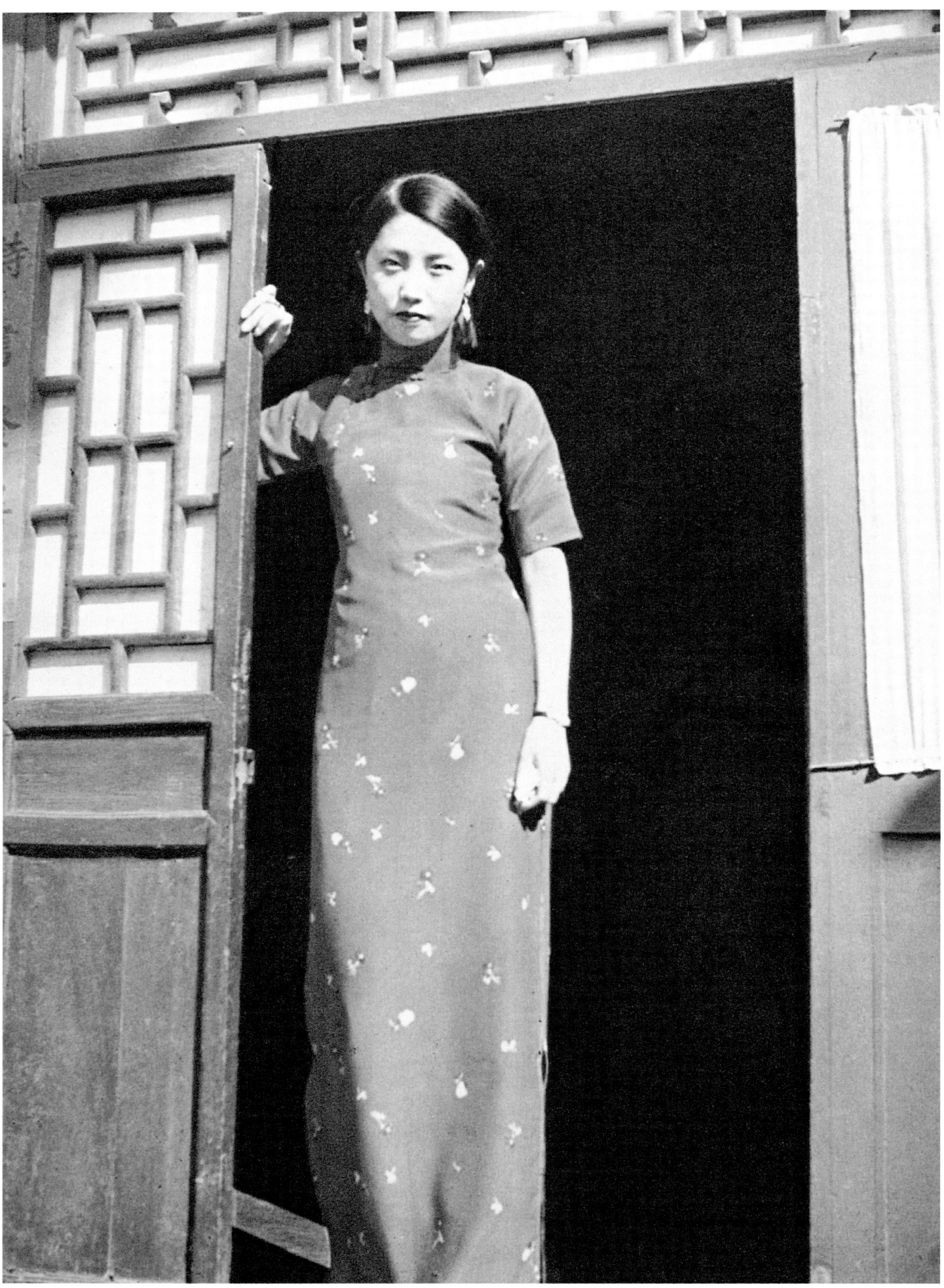

*Opposite*: A portrait of Lou, a former sing-song girl from a Peking tea house. She was the concubine of a wealthy old gentleman. This picture was taken by Ellen Thorbecke in 1934. Her photos sometimes carry the credit Ellen Catleen, her maiden name.

*Right*: A Peking cartwright practicing his ancient craft. The Chinese invention of the bowstring drill dates back to the first century BC. The manufacture of cast iron, used for bits, goes back even further. Heinz von Perckhammer took this picture in the 1920s.

*Below*: The ruins of the Summer Palace. The picture was taken by von Perckhammer almost seventy years after the palace was burnt down by Lord Elgin in retribution for the murder of the British envoys during the Arrow War.

*Above*: A young actress. Female parts were frequently played by young men and boys in traditional China. However, in the 1920s things changed dramatically and actresses often took on male roles. This sensitive photograph was taken by Heinz von Perckhammer.

*Above right*: This monk has a tiny Pekinese puppy sitting on his lap. Some Buddhists are said to believe that after monks die and are reincarnated they return to earth as dogs. Consequently, monks are very kind to these creatures. Photograph by Heinz von Perckhammer.

*Right*: A garlic street hawker shields himself from the sun beneath a battered umbrella. The Chinese were superstitious about being photographed. They believed that if they were photographed when poor, they would remain poor forever. Photograph by Heinz von Perckhammer.

# The Media Circus

The world press arrived in force to cover the Sino-Japanese War, but it was the local expatriate reporters who got the best stories. South African writer Henry John May was only 50 yards away from the Great World Amusement Palace when the bomb exploded. He wrote:

"It appeared for a moment to be about to crash, slipped sideways, then righted itself. I looked ahead up the street: a Chinese girl in a light blue dress was talking to a man—she could not have been more than twenty—and I saw, suddenly, like some dreadful surgical operation, her face blown away, leaving a gaping wound; then her body collapsed like an unpropped half-open empty bag. The man next to her had disappeared, probably blown to pieces. I saw heads flying in the air, and feet and arms, and red flames, and motor-cars enveloped in thick black smoke. I heard the dull thud of an explosion, and what seemed to be a moan from a million throats."

The most memorable scoop was by Edgar Snow. He was the first Western journalist to interview Mao Tse-tung in his cave in Yenan. At the time, Chiang Kai-shek was more interested in exterminating the Communists after the Long March than fighting the Japanese.

"I met Mao soon after my arrival: a gaunt, rather Lincolnesque figure, above average height for a Chinese, somewhat stooped, with a head of thick black hair grown very long, and with large searching eyes, a high-bridged nose and prominent cheekbones. My fleeting impression was of an intellectual face of great shrewdness."

What little was known about Mao at the time was colored by Nationalist propaganda. Snow managed, with great difficulty, to persuade Mao to talk about his early life. He heard first-hand the thoughts of Chairman Mao.

His story broke just before Chiang Kai-shek was kidnapped by the Young Marshal and forced to form a United Front with the Communists to fight the Japanese.

**The young Mao Tse-tung.** Over the last half century, this image of the Great Helmsman achieved iconic status, particularly during the Cultural Revolution, where it appeared on thousands of items which are now collected by Mao memorabilia enthusiasts.

*Right*: The scene from the Palace Hotel side of the Nanking Road looking away from the Bund. Most of the wounded and dead had been removed when this picture was taken. A car can be seen still burning in the distance.

*Below left*: A typical caravan in northern China. The most dangerous stage of Fleming and Maillart's journey was through the bleak, rugged, mountainous and ravaged region of Sinkiang where murderous bandits and deserters from rival warlord armies roamed.

*Below right*: The Japanese flagship *Idzumo* at anchor on the Whangpoo River, 14 August 1937. The journalist Henry John May took the picture half an hour before the Chinese air force attempted to bomb the warship and missed, with lethal results.

# The Lull and the Storm

It was only a matter of time before Japan launched a full-scale invasion of China and Sinophiles, sightseers, tourists and adventurers poured into the country for a last chance visit before war inevitably broke out.

Among them were Peter Fleming (the brother of Ian Fleming, the creator of James Bond) and Ella Maillart. Today they would be classified as "travel writers." In 1935, they made a hazardous journey from Peking to India through Sinkiang (Xinjiang), mainly on horseback and camel. Unlike Fleming, Maillart loathed writing, but it paid for their expenses. "We wanted to travel," wrote Fleming, "because we believed, in the light of previous experience, that we would enjoy it. We were right."

They wandered for months through bandit and warlord country, sleeping in tents and living rough. Fortunately, they both had ironclad stomachs. Keeping clean was a problem as they had only a frying pan to wash in. When they arrived eventually at Kashgar (Kashi), exhausted and in rags, they were welcomed by the British Vice-Consul, Arthur Barlow, who asked, "I don't know whether you drink beer?" Fleming noted that "he very soon did."

Two years later, even after an undeclared war was raging in the north, there were still plenty of tourists hanging around the International Settlement in Shanghai, which was in neutral territory. In spite of this, the Japanese battleship *Idzumo* was anchored a few yards north of the Soochow (Suzhou) Creek near the heart of the Bund. It was a tempting target for the Chinese air force and they attacked the Japanese fleet.

Tourists and Shanghailanders were taking tea when a stray bomb hit the luxury Palace Hotel on the Bund. Another demolished the Great World Amusement Palace and flattened a refugee camp in an unfinished building nearby. Not a single Japanese warship was hit. These air raids claimed over 2,000 innocent victims in what is today cynically called "friendly fire."

*Above*: The British Consulate at Kashgar where Peter Fleming and Ella Maillart stopped off for a few beers during their epic journey from Peking to Kashmir in British India.

*Below*: Close to the front line, Fleming casually reads a book while Mr Yao of the Central News Agency is busy writing his copy.

*Left*: A Chinese machinegun nest in the front line at Kiangwan, a village about four miles north of the International Settlement. In the battle, the Japanese destroyed almost every building, including the Shanghai Golf Clubhouse. Only one house was left standing.

*Below*: Wounded Chinese refugee women in the International Settlement. Tens of thousands of Chinese civilians poured into the concessions. The Shanghai Municipal Council, the Red Cross and the religious organizations did there best to cope with the influx.

*Opposite above*: The warships of the Japanese Imperial Navy and their land forces bombarded the Chinese municipality of Shanghai for 34 days before the Chinese forces withdrew. An estimated 18,000 Chinese civilians were killed and 240,000 homes were destroyed during the carnage.

*Opposite below left*: A Japanese salient in the Paoshan Road near the Commercial Press, the scene of the heaviest fighting. A Japanese armored car can be seen on the right. The Chinese had no anti-tank weapons and these vehicles proved invulnerable to rifle and machine-gun fire.

*Opposite below right*: The bitter fight for the Shanghai–Woosung railway line. Japanese marines can be seen in the lower right-hand corner. In the distance on the extreme left are the remains of the Commercial Press factory which was destroyed by fire.

NATIONALISTIC CHINA AT PEACE AND WAR

*Above*: The ruthless bombardment at point-blank range by Japanese warships set fire to the warehouses, factories and docks on the Pootung side of the Whangpoo River. The picture was taken by Randall Gould, editor of the *Shanghai Evening Post and Mercury*.

*Left*: Mao Tse-tung giving a lecture in 1936 after the Long March. Mao, a former schoolteacher, discussed with Edgar Snow the state of illiteracy in China and explained his plans to him for creating a people's mass-education movement to solve China's reading problem.

*Above*: General Chu Teh and his staff in Yahan. He took part in the Nanchang Uprising before joining forces with Mao Tse-tung. In 1931, he was elected Commander-in-Chief of the Red Army and together with Mao took part in the Long March in 1935.

*Below left*: "Probably the World's most grizzly and awful Tragedy" is how a contemporary writer captioned this picture. "A Chinese Aeroplane loosed two Bombs on the Square instantly annihilating a Thousand People." These words were written less than four months before the Rape of Nanking.

*Below right*: A bewildered Tibetan sits dazed on the bloodstained steps of a building on the Bund moments after the bombing raid on the morning of 14 August, 1937, when Chinese warplanes attempted to sink the Japanese warship *Idzumo*. Photograph by Henry John May.

# Bibliography

Atwell, Pamela, *British Mandarins and Chinese Reformers*, Hong Kong: Oxford University Press, 1985.

Auden, W. H. and Isherwood, Christopher, *Journey to a War*, London: Faber & Faber, 1973.

Bland, J. O., and Backhouse, E., *China Under the Empress Dowager*, London: William Heinemann, 1910.

Bonavia, David, *China's Warlords*, Hong Kong: Oxford University Press, 1995.

Bonavia, Judy, *The Yangzi River*, Hong Kong: Odyssey, 1995.

Boxer, C. R., *Fidalgos in the Far East*, London: Oxford University Press, 1968.

Chan, Charis, *Imperial China*, London: Penguin Books, 1992.

Chang, Iris, *The Rape of Nanking*, London: Penguin Books, 1997.

Coates, Austin, *China Races*, Hong Kong: Oxford University Press, 1983.

Collis, Maurice, *Foreign Mud*, London: Faber & Faber, 1956.

Collis, Maurice, *The Great Within*, London: Faber & Faber, 1941.

Crow, Carl, *400 Million Customers*, London: Hamish Hamilton, 1937.

Cunningham, Alfred, *The Chinese Soldier*, Hong Kong: Daily Press, 1899.

Denby, Jay, *Letters from China*, London: Murray & Evenden, 1911.

Drage, Charles, *General of Fortune*, London: Heinemann, 1963.

Drage, Charles, *Two-Gun Cohen*, London: Johnathan Cape, 1954.

Flemming, Peter, *One's Company*, London: Jonathan Cape, 1934.

Flemming, Peter, *The Siege at Peking*, Oxford: Oxford University Press, 1984.

Grant, Sir Hope, *Incidents of the China War of 1860*, London: William Blackwood, 1875.

Hall, W. H., *The Nemesis in China*, London: Henry Colburn, 1847.

Howard, J. Harvey, *Ten Weeks with Chinese Bandits*, New York: Dodd & Mead, 1926.

Hunter, William C., *The "Fan Kwae at Canton"*, Shanghai: Oriental Affairs, 1882.

Hurd, Douglas, *The Arrow War*, London: Collins, 1967.

Kao, George, *Chinese Wit and Humour*, New York: Sterling, 1974.

King, Paul, *In the Chinese Customs Service*, London: Heath Cranton, 1924.

Lane-Poole, Stanley, *Sir Harry Parkes in China*, London: Methuen, 1901.

Macartney, George, Earl, *An Embassy to China*, Michigan: Scholarly Press, 1972.

McAleavy, Henry, *A Dream Of Tartary*, London: George Allen & Unwin, 1963.

Menpes, Mortimer, and Blake, Sir Henry, *China*, London: Murray and Charles Black, 1909.

Morrison, G. E., *An Australian in China*, Hong Kong: Oxford University Press, 1985.

Plant, Cornell, *Glimpses of the Yangtze Gorges*, Shanghai: Kelly & Walsh, 1921.

Powell, John B., *My Twenty-Five Years in China*, New York: The Macmillian Company, 1925.

Seagrave, Sterling, *The Soong Dynasty*, London: Sidgwick & Jackson, 1985.

Singer, Aubrey, *The Lion & the Dragon*, London: Barrie & Jenkins, 1992.

Snow, Edgar, *Red Star Over China*, London: Victor Gollancz, 1937.

Soboleff, I. S. K., *Nansen Passport*, London: Bell, 1936.

Staunton, Sir George, *The Embassy to the Emperor of China*, Vol. 1, London: Stockwell, 1797.

Thomson, John, *Through China with a Camera*, London: Harper & Brothers, 1899.

Trevor-Roper, Hugh, *A Hidden Life*, London: Macmillian, 1976.

Varè, Daniele, *The Maker of Heavenly Trousers*, Guernsey: Black Swan, 1987.

Waley, Arthur, *The Opium War Through Chinese Eyes*, London: George Allen & Unwin, 1958.

Warner, Marina, *The Dragon Empress*, London: Cardinal, 1972.

Weale, B. L. Putnam, *Indiscreet Letters from Peking*, London: Hurst & Blackett, 1906.

Wei, Betty Peh-Ti, *Shanghai: Crucible of Modern China*, Hong Kong: Oxford University Press, 1987.

# Index

*Note*: Numbers in italic refer to illustrations.

A-Ma Temple, 23
Actors, 6, *147*
Actress, *266*
Advertising, 248, *249–51*
  cigarettes, 214, *214–17*
Ahong, 142
Akum, 142
Aldrich, Lucy, 230
Alexander, William, 6, *12*, 13, *26*, *43*, *44–7*, 46, 84, 87
Alexander VI, Pope, 16
Allen, J. B., 83
Allom, Thomas, 23, *90*
Amah, *221*
American Tobacco Company, 214
Americans, 94, 104, 108, 268, 280
Amherst, Lord, 19, 42
Amoy (Xiamen), 118, *118–19*
Andrãde, Simao d', 22
Anglo-Chinese trade, 32, 37
Antiques dealers, *115*
Archer, Frederick Scott, 17
Armillary sphere, 28, *28*
Armistice Parade, *12–13*
*Arrow*, 74
Arrow War, 74, 84, *91*, 92, 95, 118, 152, 166, *265*
Arthur, Capt. William, 176, *177*
Artists, *13*
Auden, W. H., 243

Backhouse, Sir Edmund, 174
Bagpipes, *178*
Bannermen, 16, 94, *95*, *106–7*
Barlow, Arthur, 272
Barnes, Lt. Col. A. A. S., 229
Battles
  Bogue, 54, *55*
  Muddy Flat, 94, *94*, 226
  Telissu, *154*
  Tsushima, 156, 176
  Yalu River, 152
Beggar, *84*
Belgians, *137*
Bell Tower, *115*

Bewick, Thomas, *33*
Bible reading, *100*
Bing Di, Emperor, *71*
Bird, Isabella, *132*, *204*
Black Dragon Society, 258, 268
Bland, J. O., 174
Blücher, Marshal, 268
Bonham, Sir George, 68, 69, 72
Borget, Auguste, *58–61*, *71*
Borodin, Michael, 196
Bowlby, Mr, 74
Bowring, Sir John, 74
Boxer Rebellion, 20, 155, 170, *170–3*
Boy Scouts, *242*, 243
Breakfast, *179*
Bremer, Sir J. J. Gordon, 102, *103*
Britain/British, 20, 152, 158
  attack on Manchus, 94
  attacks on Canton, 64, 74
  capture of Shanghai, 64
  consulate, Canton, *120*
  consuls, 118
  extraterritorial rights, 118
  Hankow, 234
  Opium War, 64
  spies, 258
  Weihaiwei, 155, 158, 196
British–American Tobacco Company, 214
Brothels, 99
Brown, Eliphalet Jr, *8*, 9
Brown, Margaret H., *279*
Bruce, Frederick, 75
Bry, Théodore de, *78*
Burgevine, Henry, 108, *109*
Burma, 152

Camels, *135*, *189*
  sculptures, *9*
Camões, Luis de, 24, *24*, 25
Campbell, Colin, 38, *38*
Canals, *45–7*, *163*
Canning, Capt. L. E., 227
*Canque*, *181*
Canton (Guangzhou), 20, *32–5*, *98–9*, *120*, *121*, *198–9*

allied headquarters, 77
Botanical Gardens, 223
British attacks, 64, 74
British consulate, 120
Bund, *225*
factories, *39*, 55, 58, *58*, 61, 118, *121*
Flowery Pagoda, *223*
foreign traders, 16, 32
rebellion, 184
River, *179*
Caravan, *273*
Cartes-de-visite, *141*
Cartoons, 94, *113*, 182, *182*, *183*, *212–13*, 232, 248, *253*, 254, 256, *256*, *257*
Carts, *44*, *132*
Cartwright, 265
Castiglione, Giuseppe, 84
Catherine of Braganza, 128
Catherine the Great, 42
Catleen, Ellen, *see* Thorbecke, Ellen
Chang, Iris, 278
Chang, Mr, *148*, 149
Chang Hsueh-liang (Zhang Xueliang), 238, *240*, 241, 274
Chang Tso-lin (Zhang Zuolin), 196, *199*, 208, *209*, 230, 238
Chang Tsung-chang (Zhang Zongchang), 208, *209*
Chao Kung, Abbot, *see* Lincoln, Trebitsch
Chaochow, 142
Chapdelaine, Abbé, 92
Charles I, King, 22
Chen, Eugene, 234
Cheng Ho (Zheng He), 68
Cheng I-sao (Mrs Cheng), 68, *68*
Cheng Tung (Zhengtong), Emperor, 68
Chengtu (Chengdu), 198
Chess, 164, *165*
Chia Ching (Jianqing), Emperor, 42, 48
Chiang Kai-shek, 196, 200, 222, 230, 234, *234*, 236,

238, *240*, 241, 243, 268, 274, 278, 280
Chiang Kai-shek, Madame, *see* Soong Mei-ling
Chien Lung (Qianlong), Emperor, 20, 42, *43*, 92
China ponies, *137*, 150, *209*
Chinese Religious Tract Society leaflet, *101*
Chinese Revolution, 94
Ching (Qing) dynasty, 16, 92–4, 106, 184
Ching-shan, 174
Chinkiang, 65
Chinnery, George, 58, *101*
Chopsticks, *180*
Chou En-lai (Zhou Enlai), 234, *235*, 241
Chu Mao-ju, 230
Chu Teh (Zhu De), 241, *276*, 280
Chuenpee (Chuanbi), 62, *63*
Chun, Prince, *153*, 154, 156, 184
Chun Ling Soo, *121*
Chung Chen (Chongzhen), Emperor, 16
Chungking (Chongqing), 118, 202, 208, 236, *240*, 241, 282
Church of St Paul, *25*, 28
Chusan (Zhoushan), 62
Clark, Bobby, 222
Clubs, *127*, 150, *150–1*, 188
Co-hong merchants, 20, 32, 38, *41*, 54
Cohen, Morris, 222, *222*, *224*, 258
Communist Party, 196, 234
Concessions, 155–6, 158, 176, 198
Conseequa's house, *41*
Convention of Peking, 20
Country Trade, 48
Court scene, *221*
Creelman, James, 155
Crow, Carl, 230, 248
Cunningham, Alfred, 152
Cunningham, Edward, 94
Customs House, *111*
Customs Service, 110, 188

Dadu (Peking), 44
Dailey, Charles, 234
Dairen (Dalian), 155, 176, 282
Delano, Warren Jr., 48
Denby, Jay, 182
Dent, Lancelot, 48
Derby, Lord, 20
Double Tenth 1911, 184
Drage, Charles, 202
Dragon Throne, 152
Drake, Sir Francis, 32
Duke, James "Buck", 214
Dutch, 16, 22

East India Companies, 32
   Dutch, 16, 32, 38
   English, 16, 19, 20, 32, 35, 37, 38, 48, 54, 100
   Swedish, 32, 38, *39*, *40*
East India House, 37
*Eastern Sketch, The*, 182, *182–3*, 256
Eight Banners, *107*
El Pinal, 22
Elgin, Lord, 74, *74*, *75*, *77*, 155, *265*
Elizabeth, Queen, 32
Elliot, Capt. Charles, 62, *63*, 64, 103
Elliot, Capt. R., *88*
Encarnacao, M., 111
Engravings, 12–13
Erben, Hermann, 268, *269*
Ever-Victorious Army, 95, 108
Expatriates
   boys, *181*
   life, 178, *181*

Falkenhausen, General von, 278
Family groups, *17*, *18*, *181*, 253
Fashions, 138, *138–41*, *252–5*
Feng Yu-hsiang (Feng Yuxiang), 158, 196, *199*, 206, *207*, 238
Fengdu, 202
Films, *252*
Fleming, Peter, *272*, *272*, *273*
Flynn, Errol, 268, *269*
Foochow (Fuzhou), 118, 128, *129*
Footbinding, 138, *138*
Foreign policy, China, 19–20, 92
France/French
   concessions, 152, 158, 196, 259
   forces, 95
   missionaries, 92
   Shanghai, 92, 108, 259, *259*, 268
Francis Xavier, St, 22, 25, 92
Fuling, 202
Fushan, 108

Gamages Emporium, 178
Gaselee, Sir Alfred, 170, *171*
George III, King, 20, 42, 92
Germany/Germans, 118, 155, 158, 258
   Embassy, *193*
Giorgio, Ludovico, 80
Girls, *164*, *181*
Glebov, General, 232
Goble, Jonathan, 132, 134
Golfers, *151*
Gordon, Charles "Chinese", 95, 108, *108*, 118
Gordon Hall, *127*
Gough, Sir Hugh, 19, 64, *64*
Gould, Randall, *275*, *279*
Grand Canal, 44, *45–7*, 64, *260*
Grandfather, *164*
Grant, Gen. Sir Hope, 74
*Graphic, The*, 84
Great China Tea Race, 128, *128–9*
Great Game, 152, 155
Great Leap Forward, 282
Great Tobacco War, 214
Great Wall of China, *4–5*, 208, *210–11*
Great World Amusement Palace, 212, *277*
Green Gang, 196, 234, *235*, 258
Grimble, H., 118
Grotto of Camões, *24*, 25
Guinness, Geraldine, *100*
Guinness, H. Grattan, 99
Gutzlaff, Karl, 100, *102*, *103*

Hadamen Gate, *2*, 4
Hairstyles, 180, *181*
Hall, Capt. Basil, 78, 82
Hankow (Hankou), *186*, 200, 234
Harbin, 198, 232
Hart, Sir Robert, 110, *110*, 111, 188, *188*, 218
Hawkers, *60*, 244, *266*
Hayashi, Yukichi, 280
Hayter, H. W. G., 182, *182*, *183*
Heard, Augustine, 48
Heavenly Kingdom of Great Peace, 104
Heine, William, *23*, *24*, 25
Hermann, Dr Emmanuel, 218
Hildebrandt, Edward, *27*
Hing, A., *141*
HMS *Actaeon*, 70
HMS *Cleopatra*, *72–3*
HMS *Medea*, *69*
HMS *Vindictive*, *236*
Honan Island, *179*
Hondius, Jodocus, 78, *79*
Hondt, Henricus, 78
Hondt, Josse de, *see* Hondius, Jodocus

Hong Kong, 62, 63, 64, 68, 118, 158
   Volunteers, 268
Honourable East India Company, *see* East India Company: English
Hope, Adm. Sir James, 105
Hopkirk, Peter, 198
Hoppo, 32, 38
Horse-racing, 150, *150*, 280, *281*
Hotsumi, Ozaki, 258
Houseboats, *133*
Houses, *96–7*
Howard, Harvey, 230, *230*
Hsien Feng (Xianfeng), Emperor, 74, 166, 168
Hsui Tsai-ying, *254*
Hundred Days, 155
Hung Hsiu-chuan (Hong Xiuquan), 92, 104, *104*, 105
Hung Wu (Hongwu), 92
Hunter, William, 58, *60*, 100
Huygens, Christiaan, 178

I-ching, 19
Ichang (Yichang), 118, 150
*Illustrated London News*, 13, *13*, 84
Imperial Drainage Canal, 170, *171*
Imperial Maritime Customs, 110, 188
Imperial Palace, *112*
Imperial Tobacco Company, 214
Innes, James, 48
Interlopers, 48, 54
Iquan, Nicholas, 68
Isherwood, Christopher, 243

Japan/Japanese
   Bluejackets, *15*
   Korea, 152, 200, 238
   Liaodong Peninsula, 158, 200
   Manchuria, 200, 238
   military, *154*, 155, 258, 268, *269*, *270*, 278
   Mukden, 238
   pirates, 22
   Port Arthur, 200, 238
   Russo-Japanese War, 176, 200
   Shanghai, 241, 268, *270*, *272*, *273*, *275*, 278
   Shantung, 196, 200
   Sino-Japanese War, 155–6, 158, 200
   Taiwan, 158, 200
   train explosions, 238
   Tsingtao, 196, 238
   warships, *270*, *273*
   Weihaiwei, 206
Japanese Company, 229

Jardine, William, 48, *50*, 54, 100
Jehol (Cheng-de), *168*
Jesuits, 25, *28*, *28–30*, 78
Jih Pen-tzu, *231*
John Company, *see* East India Company: English
Johnston, Sir Reginald, 158, *159*, 206, *207*
Jui-Lin, *146*, 147
Junks, 46, *60*, *70*, *124*, 132, *135*, *144–5*, *164*

Kang Hsi (Kangxi), Emperor, *28*, *30*, 32, 35
Kang Yu-wei (Kang Youwei), 94, 155, 166
Kawashima, Yoshiko, 238, *239*
Keay, Captain, 128
Kelly, Captain, 94, *94*
Keswick, John, 258
Keswick, William, 258, 280
Kiangnan (Jiangnan), 226
Kiangsi (Jiangxi) Soviet, 241
Kidnappings, 230
King, Paul, 150, 188, *190*
Kirkpatrick, Sir George, 228
Kishen (Qishan), 62, 64
Kiukiang Bund, *190–1*
Komarov, N. V., 152
Korea, 152, 155, 200
Koxinga (Guoxingye), 68, *71*
Kuang Hsu (Guangxu), Emperor, 112, 155, 156, 166, 184
Kublai Khan, 16, 44, 46, 68, *71*, 112
Kuhn & Komor, 218
Kung, H. H., 223, 241
Kung (Gong), Prince, 166, *167*
Kuo Shou-ching (Guo Shoujing), 28, *28*
Kuo Sung-tao, *183*
Kuomintang (Guomindang), 196, 234, 258
Kwan, Admiral, 62
Kwanchowan, 196

Lama Temple, *194*
Lantern painter's shop, *90*
Lao She, 252
Lay, G. T., 118
Lay, Horatio Nelson, 110, 111
Le Breton Bedwell, Frederic, *105*
Li, Maj.-Gen., K. Y., *231*
Li, Prince, 104, 108
Li Chien-nung, 92
Li Hung-chang (Li Hongzhang), 108, *108*, *124*, 152, 158, 166
Li Yuan-hung (Li Yuanhong), 184, *186*, *187*, 196, 200

*Above*: Most of the bodies had been removed when this picture of the Great World Amusement Palace bombing was taken. Henry John May described vividly how "the dead were piled into lorries, thrown into them like so many mutilated carcasses of animals."

*Left*: May was knocked over by a bomb blast a few minutes after he took this photograph of a tiny canvas eating-house on a wharf near the Japanese warship *Idzumo*. All the Chinese coolies in this picture were killed by the bomb.

# The Rape of Nanking (December 1937)

The Japanese captured Shanghai in 1937 and thousands of Chinese refugees fled across Garden Bridge from the Japanese-controlled sector of the International Settlement into neutral ground, which was guarded by British, American and French troops.

Japan's next objective was Nanking which had replaced Peking as the capital of China. Chiang Kai-shek hurriedly left the city and commanded General Tang to defend the capital to the last man. Three days later, when it was surrounded by Japanese forces, Chiang ordered Tang to abandon the city. To retreat, Tang's armies had to cross the Yangtze River. Tang and a few of his men were able to escape. The rest were left to their doom.

The Chinese soldiers who surrendered outnumbered the victorious Japanese. The prisoners were systematically executed. The victors entered Nanking and went berserk. They slaughtered, raped, tortured, beheaded and buried alive over 300,000 people.

In Nanking, the foreign residents had set up an International Safety Zone and had hung Red Cross banners around the perimeter. The Japanese military did not officially recognize it, but the killing, rapine, and looting was far less in the zone. Iris Chang in her book, *The Rape of Nanking*, wrote, "The zone eventually accommodated some 200,000–300,000 refugees—almost half the Chinese population left in the city."

She records the horror of the massacre in appalling detail. Chang also tells of the bravery of the International Safety Zone Committee and their colleagues. They were frequently beaten up, abused and their homes looted. The head of the committee was John Rabe, a German businessman, who was paradoxically also the leader of Nanking's Nazi Party. In spite of his politics, he was a humane man, absolutely fearless and a brilliant organizer. During those terrible days, the committee did everything in their power (which was almost negligible) to protect and feed the refugees. What they lacked in real power was made up for by their unshakeable tenacity and indomitable heroism.

Chinese troops at a rally in Nanking. These men of the 87th and 88th Model Divisions were trained by German General von Falkenhausen's Military Mission. Many of them were captured by the Japanese and subsequently butchered in cold blood.

*Opposite*: The Chairman of the Communist Party of China, Mao Tse-tung, announces the founding of the People's Republic of China at Tiananmen Square in Peking on 1 October 1949. Chiang Kai-shek and his defeated Nationalist government fled to Taiwan.

*Below*: A papercut of a Communist soldier. The Chinese have been making papercuts since the first century AD. This highly skilled folk craft was adapted successfully into Soviet art.

*Below left*: The slogans on the blackboard urge workers to learn from the revolution, increase production, work hard and prepare for war. This graphic was produced during the Great Leap Forward, a disastrous economic policy.

*Below right*: During the Great Leap Forward, Mao dictated that all art should serve the revolution. The slogan encourages the proletariat to study books and have a thorough understanding of Marxism.

launched a partially successful Five Year Plan before initiating his Great Leap Forward in 1958, which resulted in years of famine. This was followed by the Cultural Revolution. China became an almost totally isolated country until President Nixon visited the country in 1972.

After Mao's death in 1976, the Gang of Four were arrested, Teng Hsiao-ping (Deng Xiaoping) took control and China began to open up again to the outside world. Teng established a number of market economy-oriented Special Economic Zones. They are the quasi-treaty ports of today where many foreign traders live an isolated life in luxury hotels or foreign enclaves. The situation is somewhat similar to the Canton factories and the treaty ports of bygone days. Extraterritorial rights and the foreign control of treaty ports were abrogated by mutual agreement in London in 1943; however, expatriates in today's China are unofficially protected from the full rigors of Chinese law, as they were in the Ching dynasty.

A large majority of the old treaty ports have flourished. Shanghai is China's wealthiest city again; Chungking has the largest population in the country, and Dairen (Dalian), which was only a few mud huts in 1860, is now the most magnificent city in Manchuria.

*Left*: During the Sino-Japanese War, expatriate racing enthusiasts continued holding race meetings in the treaty ports. The last meeting was held in Tientsin on the eve of Pearl Harbor. Racing did not resume in Shanghai after World War II.

*Below*: Paper hunts were a sporting feature from the earliest days of the treaty ports. They were popular with the expatriate community because ladies were allowed to compete. The Japanese allowed these hunts to continue in some areas under their military control.

# Epilogue

After the Rape of Nanking, life became difficult for foreigners in the treaty ports. With the outbreak of World War II in Europe, things got worse.

The treaty ports were still technically neutral. The Japanese tried to rig the Shanghai Municipal Council elections, but the British and Americans were more experienced at rigging elections and outsmarted them. The chairman of the Japanese Ratepayers' Association, Yukichi Hayashi, was so incensed that he shot and wounded William Keswick, the British chairman of the council, at a public meeting held at the racecourse.

Racing continued at the treaty ports and the Japanese even allowed the odd paper-hunt outside the settlements, but a Japanese officer had to be present to prevent incidents. The only incident recorded was when Major Oka fell off his horse. The last horse race was held at Tientsin, the day before Pearl Harbor.

Allied civilians were thrown into concentration camps, but neutrals, White Russians and citizens of the Axis powers had to cope somehow with living in occupied China. Many died. Trebitsch Lincoln, who had escaped being executed by the British and Germans for treason, was among those murdered by the Japanese.

In 1945, the war ended when the Americans dropped atomic bombs on Hiroshima and Nagasaki, where 210,000 Japanese died. This is less than the 300,000 Chinese butchered by General Iwane Matsui's forces in Nanking in 1937. If you include the Chinese killed by Japanese during this bloody campaign, the number of victims increases dramatically. Nanking was not the only place put to the sword.

Soviet Russia declared war on Japan just before the end of World War II and occupied Manchuria and Mongolia. Civil war broke out again between the Nationalists and the Communists and Mao Tse-tung established the People's Republic of China in 1949. Chiang Kai-shek fled to Taiwan and set up an alternative Nationalist Government on the island.

Chairman Mao established a Communist state and

*Above*: Japanese bombers over Shansi in 1939, where Chu Teh's Communist Red Army and Yen Hsi-shan's Nationalist New Shansi Army were fighting a largely guerrilla war against the invaders, instead of against each other.

*Below*: General Iwane Matsui, commander-in-chief of the Imperial Japanese Army at Nanking.

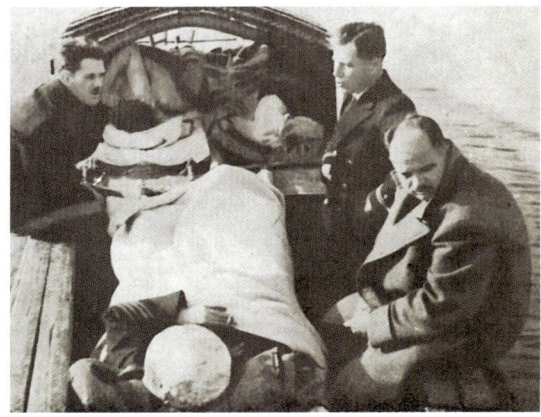

*Left*: The surgeon and three casualties escape in a sampan from the USS *Panay*, a neutral American gunboat sunk by Japanese bombers. The photograph was taken by one of the surviving civilian passengers, Eric Mayell, of *Fox Movietone News*.

*Below left*: Thousands of refugees pour over Garden Bridge into the safe haven of Shanghai's International Settlement, which was neutral ground. Photograph by Randall Gould, editor of the *Shanghai Evening Post and Mercury*.

*Above right*: The cover of Margaret H. Brown's novel *Heaven Knows*. Brown witnessed first hand the terrible suffering of the Chinese civilian population.

*Below right*: Nationalist flags fly defiantly over Nanking's Drum Tower, silhouetted against the burning city. This anti-war protest cover appeared on *The China Journal*.

Liao Chung-Kai, *222*
Liaodong Peninsula, 155, 158, 176, 200
Liddell, N. O., 94
Lin, Commissioner, 62, *62*
Lin Yutang, 208
Lincoln, Trebitsch, 200, 258, *258*, 280
Lintin Island, 48, *50–1*
Little, Archibald, 205
Liukung (Liugong) Island, *159–61*
Lockhart, Sir James Stewart, 158
Lockyer, Captain, *69*
London Missionary Society, 92, 100, 102, *103*, 138
Long March, 241, *242*
Lord's Prayer, *101*
Lou, 264, *264*
Lu Hsun, 255
Lung Yu (Longyu), Empress, *166*

Ma Jui, 208
Ma Yue, *14*
Macartney, Lord, 19, 42, *42*, *43*, 44
Macau, 16, 22–4, 27–8, 78
MacDonald, Sir Claude, 170, 182, *182*
Magic lantern, 178, *180*, *181*
Mah Sam, 222
Maillart, Ella, 272, *273*
Malacca, 22
Manchukuo, 238
Manchuria, 155, 198, 200, 238, 241, 280, 282
Manchus, 16, *18*, 68, 74, 94, 95, 104, 108, 152, 156, 184
 women, 138, *140*
Mandarins, *11*, 32, *36*, 42, 48, 54, 58, 87, 110, 118
 traveling boat, *47*
Mao Tse-tung (Mao Zedong), 156, 239, 241, *242*, *274*, *275*, 280, 282, *283*
Maps
 China, 78, *79–83*
 Macau and Taipa, *22*
 Shanghai, *243*
Marco Polo Bridge Incident, *240*, 241
Martial arts, *190*
Mason, Major George Henry, *52*, 84
Matheson, James, 48, *50*
Matsui, Iwane, 280, *280*
May, Henry John, 274, *277*
May the Fourth Movement, 196
Mayell, Eric, *279*
McEuen, Capt. J. P., 94, *95*
Mennie, Donald, 202, *203*, 205, 260, *260–3*

Menpes, Mortimer, 162, *162–5*
Merchant, *141*
Mesquita, Vicente Nicolau de, 27
Miller, Milton M., *11*, *12*, *17*, *18*
Milton, John, *44*
Min River, *124*
Ming dynasty, 22, 92
Ministers of State, *93*, 94
Missionaries, 92, 99, 100, *100–3*, 170, *171*
Moneychanger, *52*
Mongolia/Mongols, 16, 138, 198, 280
Monk, *266*
Morrison, G. E., 174, *174*, *175*, 182
Morrison, Robert, 92, 100, *101*
Mother-in-law, *267*
Mourning trumpeters, *263*
Mukden, 238
Muravyov-Amursky Peninsula, 152
Murphy, R. C., 94
Muslim rebellions, 92

Nanking (Nanjing)
 Arsenal, *124–5*
 Britain, 64
 Drum Tower, *279*
 Japanese, 241
 Koxinga, 68, *71*
 Nationalist capital, 196, 240
 Rape of, 243, 278
 Taipings, *104–6*
Nansen, Fridtjof, *233*
Nansen Passport, 232, *233*
Napier, Lord, 54, 58, 62, 100
Napoleon, Bonaparte, 19
National Revolution Army, 234
*Nemesis*, 19, *21*
New Life Movement, 243
Nicholas II, Tsar, 176
Nievhoff, John, *33*, *112*
Nineteenth Route Army, 268, *268*
Ningpo (Ningbo), 18, 19, 64, *65*, 118
Niuhuru (Ci An), Empress, *166*
Nogi, General, *154*
Northern Expedition, 196, 200, 234

O'Callaghan, Captain, 94, *94*
O'Connor, Martins, 192, *192*
Opium, 20, 48, *48*, *49*, 58, 62
 War, 16, 20, *62–5*, 64
Ortelius, Abraham, *80–1*, 82
Paddle steamers, 19, *19*, *21*, *69*

Pak Shan Lan, 27
Palmer, William, 230
Palmerston, Lord, 54, 63, 64, 74
Parkes, Harry, 74, *75*, 77, 118, *121*, 226
Peel, Sir Robert, 20, 54
Peking (Beijing), *10*
 antique trade, 244
 Bell Tower, *115*
 Chang Tso-lin, 238
 Chinese City, 112, *113*, *115*
 Feng Yu-hsiang, 196
 Forbidden City, *12–13*, *113*, *114*, 206
 Hsi Pien Men Gate, *195*
 imperial palace, *112*
 Kublai Khan, 44
 Legation Quarter, *193*
 map, *113*
 observatory, *30–1*
 Railway Station, *136–7*
 siege, 170, *170–3*
 Tartar Wall, *172–3*
 Temple of Heaven, *116–17*
 White Lotus, 94
 Yen Hsi-shan, 238
Peng, Maj. Gen. C. S., *231*
Perckhammer, Heinz von, 15, 260, *265–7*
Perry, Commodore Matthew, 23
Photographers/photographic techniques, 13–14, 260
Pirates, 68, *68–73*
Plant, Cornell, *204*
Plant seller, 84, *85*
Poker, *248*, 248
Polo, Marco, 16, *46*, 112
Porcelain Tower, *105*
Port Arthur (Lushun), 155, 156, 158, 176, *177*, 200, 238
Port Edward, 158
Portuguese, 16, 22, 27, 42
Postcards, *113*, 218, *218–21*
Pottinger, Sir Henry, 64, *64*, 105
Powell, John B., 230, 238
Prints: China, 84
Pu Ju, *175*
Pu Qua, 52, *84–5*
Pu Yi (Puyi), Emperor, *153*, 154, 156, 158, 184, *185*, 196, 206, *207*, 238, 239
Putnam Weale, B. L., 155, 176, 182, 234

Rabe, John, 278
Rapkin, John, *83*
Red Army, 241
Red boats, 261, *261*
Reform Movement, 94, 155, 166
Refugees, *271*, 279

Rhoades, Randall, 218
Ricalton, James, *179*
Ricci, Matteo, 28, *29*, 78
Rickshaw, 132, *134*, *262*
Roberts, Reverend Issachar, 92, 104, 105
Royal Navy, 18, *18*, 19, *19*, 21, 54, *55*, 62, *160–1*
Rozhestvensky, Admiral, 176
Russia/Russians
 advisers, 196, 234
 fleet, 156, *176*, *177*
 Liaodong Peninsula, 155, 158, 176, 200
 Muravyov-Amursky Peninsula, 152
 spy network, 258
 White, 198, 212, 226, 232, *232*, *233*, 280
Russo-Japanese War, *154*, 155, 156, *156*, 176, 200
Rustichello, 16

Sahlgren, Nicholas, 38
Salt merchant's house, *61*
Saltoun, Lord, 19, *65*, *66*
Sam, 255
Samfoo, 138, *139*
Sampans, *132*
Sapajou, *232*, *248*, *256*, 256
Sapojnikov, Georgi, *see* Sapajou
Sassoon, Sir Victor, 208
Satire, 182
Schall, Adam, 28
Schiff, Friedrich, *113*, 212–13, 256, *257*
Scholars, *141*, *163*
Scidmore, Eliza R., 112
Scott, Sir George Gilbert, *102*
Second Revolution, 226, 229
Second United Front, 241
Sedan chairs, 132, *135*
Sentinel of the South, 202, *202*
Shadow boxing, 218, *219*
Shamien (Shameen), 118, *120–1*, *224–5*
Shangchuan, 22
Shanghai
 Anglo-American defence, 94–5
 Bund, *123*, 218, *245–7*
 capture by Britain, 64
 capture by Small Swords, 94, 108, 110
 Cathedral, *102*
 Chiang Kai-shek, 196, 230, 234
 Chinese City, 234
 Chinese refugees, 198, 244
 Club, 150, *151*
 Communists, 234
 customs collection, 110
 Defence Force, 226, *236*, *237*

Foochow Road, *244*
French Concession, 92, *259*
Garden Bridge, *236-7*
Hongkong and Shanghai Bank building, *245*, *247*
International Settlement, 92, 94, 95, 234, *236-7*, 244, 272, 279
Japanese attacks, 241, 268, 260, *268-71*
Manchus, 94
Municipal Council, 92, 94-5, 182, 226, 258, 280
Municipal Police, 94, 95, 232, *259*
Nanking Road, 200, *122*, *201*
nightlife, 212, *212*, *213*
population, 198, 200, 212
Regiment Horse Artillery, *227*
Small Swords, 94, 108
South Station, *267*
spies, 258
Taiping threat, 104
treaty port, 118
Volunteer Corps, 94, 226, *226-9*, 268, *269*
walled city, 94, 108, *123*, *247*
War, *15*
White Russians, 232
Willow Tea House, *131*
Will's Bridge, *122*
Shansi (Shanxi), 198, *280*
Shantung, 196, 200
Shisanhanglu, 38, *39*
Shun Chih (Shunzhi), Emperor, *18*
Sian Incident, 241
Sikh policeman, *126*, 127
Silk, 32, 38, *41*
Silver, 48
Sing-song girls, *254*, *264*, 265
Sino-Japanese War, *154*, 155, 158, 166, 200, 274
Small Swords, 94, 108, 110
Smedley, Agnes, 258, *258*
Smith, Capt. Henry, 62
Smugglers, 48
Smythe, Sir Thomas, 35
Snow, Edgar, 274, *275*
Snow, Miss, *254*
Soboleff, Kralichek, 232, *233*
Society of Righteous and Harmonious Fists, 170
Soldiers, *12*, *240*, *271*, *278*, *282*
Soochow (Suzhou) bridge, *47*
Soong, Charlie, 94, 223, 241
Soong, T. A., 243
Soong, T. L., 243
Soong, T. V., 243
Soong Ai-ling (Song Ailing), 223, 241

Soong Ching-ling (Song Qingling), 222, *222*, 223, 241, *253*
Soong Mei-ling (Song Meiling), 223, 230, 241, *241*, 242
Sorge, Richard, 258, *258*
Spanish, 16, 22
Special Economic Zones, 282
Speed, John, 78, *82*
Spice trade, 32, 35
Spies, 258
SS *Hung-Fu*, 205
SS *Leechuen*, 205
Stanfield, William Clarkson, *88-9*
Staunton, George (father), 42, *43*, 58, 100
Staunton, George (son), 42, *43*, 100
Stephan, Heinrich von, 218
Stereoscopes, 178, *179*
Sternberg, M., *221*
Stirling, Admiral, 94
Stoessel, General, *154*
Stone Boat, *43*
Straw coats, *46*
Su, Prince, 238
Summer Palace (Yuanmingyuan), 28, 74, 75, *114-15*, 155, *265*
new, 166, *169*
Sun Tzu, 16, *20*, *21*, 64
Sun Yat-sen, 94, 156, *156*, 184, *187*, 196, *197*, 198, 202, 222, *222*, 223, 234, 241, *253*
Sung-chiang, 108
Sutton, Frank, 208, *208*
Szechwan (Sichuan), 92

Tai Li (Dai Li), 258
Taipans, 48, 62
Taiping Rebellion, 74, 77, 92, 94, 104, 152, 226
Taipings, 94, 95, 104, *105-6*, 108
Taiwan (Formosa), 68, 71, 158, 200
Tallis, John, *83*
Tanaka, Ryukichi, 238
Tang, General, 278
Tao Kuang (Daoguang), Emperor, 62, *63*
Tea, 38, 40, *53*, *128*
garden, *130*
merchant, *99*
-tasting room, *131*
Temple of Heaven, *116-17*
Teng Hsiao-ping (Deng Xiaoping), 282
Teng Ting-chen (Deng Tingzhen), 62
Thom, Robert, 118
Thomson, John, *9*, *93*, 94, 112, *115*, 138, *138*, 142, *142-9*
Thorbecke, Ellen, 263, *265*, 267
Three Gorges, 202, *202-5*, *261*, *263*
Tibetan, 277
Lama, *221*
Tientsin (Tianjin), 118, *126-7*, 196, 200, *254*
Tiger Island, *88-9*
Tigers of War, *18*
Ting, Admiral, 152, *159*
Tinghai, 62
Titus, Calvin P., *172*
Togo, Admiral, *176*
Tomlinson, Colonel, *66-7*
Tourists, 272
Tradesman, *26*, *27*, *143*
Trains/railways, 132, *134*, 222, *231*
Transport, 132
Treaty of
Nanking, 64, 92
Tientsin (Tianjin), 75
Tordesillas, 16
Whampoa, 92
Treaty ports, 74, 95, 99, 118, 243, 244, *253*, 280, 282
Trevor-Roper, Hugh, 174
Triads, 92, 94
Tsai Ting-kai (Cai Tingkai), Gen., 268
Tsai Ying, *175*
Tseng Kuo-fan (Zeng Guofan), 108, 152
Tsingtao (Qingdao), 118, *118*, *119*, 155, 158, 196, 200, 238
Tu Yueh-sheng (Du Yuesheng) (Big-Eared Tu), 196, 212, 230, 234, *235*
Tung Chih (Tongzhi), Emperor, 166
Tzu Hsi (Cixi), Empress Dowager, 112, *113*, 152, 155, 156, *157*, 166, *166*, *167*, 184

Ungern-Sternberg, Baron, 198, *200*
United Front, 234
United States, 196, 282
Army, *235*
Marines, *237*
Urga (Hurae), 198
USS *Panay*, 279

Varè, Bettina, 192, *192*
Varè, Daniele, 152, 192, *195*
Verbiest, Ferdinand, 28, *30*
Victoria, Queen, 77
Vladivostok, 152
*Wako*, 22
Wan Hsien (Wanxian), 202, *202*, 204

Wan Jung (Wanrong), *207*, 238, *239*
Wan Li (Wanli), Emperor, 78
Wanping, 240
War artists, 13, 84, *91*
War junks, 19, *21*
Ward, Frederick Townsend, 95, 108, *109*
Ward, Sir Leslie, *183*
Washington Conference, 158, 196, 200
Weddell, John, 22
Weddings, *253*
Wei, Katherine, 252
Weihaiwei (Weihai), 152, 155, 158, *158-61*, 196, 206
Weldon, C. D., *130*
Wellington, Duke of, 54
Westernized Chinese, 252, *253*
Whampoa, 55, *56-7*
Military Academy, 196, *234*
Wheelbarrow Riots, 226
Wheelbarrows, 132, *133*
Whistler, James McNeill, 162
White, Lieutenant, *23*, *63*
White Lotus Society, 92, 94
White Terror, 234
Wilhelm II, Kaiser, 155, 158
William IV, King, 54
Willow Tea House, *131*
Winter Palace, *168*
Women, *17*, *18*, 98, 138, *138-41*, 252
Wong, "Newsreel", 260, 267
Wong Jen-mei, *255*
Wood engravings, *3*, *91*
Woosung (Wusong), 232
World War I, 196, 200
World War II, 243, 280
Wray, A. H., *83*
Wu Pei-fu (Wu Peifu), 196, 208, *209*
Wuchang, 184, *184*, *186*
Wuchow (Wuzhou) Customs House, *191*
Wuhan, 234

Yang, Captain, *148*, 149
Yang, Madame, 252
Yang, Mr, 142, *143*
Yang-chau (Yangzhou), *46*
Yang Fang (banker), 108
Yang Fang, Gen., 19
Yang Sen, 198, 208
Yangtze River, 202
Yao, Mr, *272*
Yen Hsi-shan (Yan Xishan), 198, 238, 280
Yuan Shih-kai (Yuan Shikai), 155, *156*, 184, *187*, 196, 198, 229
Yung Cheng (Yongzheng), Emperor, 48